DO IT LIKE A PILOT

Leadership, Communication, Teamwork and Management Skills.

From the Ground Up.

Do it Like a Pilot. . Leadership, Communication, Teamwork and Management Skills. From the Ground Up is the eighth book by Owen Zupp. His first book, 'Down to Earth', was published in 2006 by Grub Street (UK), while his title, 'Without Precedent' has been even more widely acclaimed. An award-winning aviation writer, his work has been featured in magazines across the globe including Fly Past (UK), Airliner World (UK), Aviation History (US), Plane & Pilot (US), Global Aviator (South Africa) and Australian Aviation. Owen has won Australasian Aviation Press Club awards and is a commercial pilot with more than 30 years' experience.

www.owenzupp.com

DO IT LIKE A PILOT

Owen Zupp

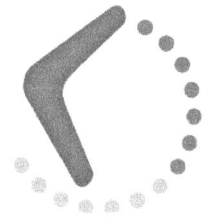

Copyright (c) Owen Zupp 2020

First published in 2020.

Registered Office P.O. Box 747, Bowral NSW 2576. Australia.

Author: Zupp, Owen 1964-

Title: DO IT LIKE A PILOT. Leadership, Communication, Teamwork and Management Skills. From the Ground Up.

By Owen Zupp

ISBN. 978-0-9946038-5-2

Subjects: Strategy. Management. Leadership.

All rights reserved. No part of this document may be reproduced, stored in a retrieval system, or transmitted in any form or by any means electronic, mechanical, photocopying, recording or otherwise without the permission of the copyright owner.

Back Cover Image by Anthony Jackson.

Also, by Owen Zupp.

The Practical Pilot. (Paperback and eBook)

Boeing 747. Queen of the Skies. Reflections from the Flight Deck. (Paperback and eBook)

'Without Precedent' Fighter Pilot, Commando. (Hardcover, Paperback and eBook)

'50 Tales of Flight' (Paperback and eBook)

'50 More Tales of Flight' (Paperback and eBook)

'Solo Flight' One Pilot's Aviation Adventure around Australia (Paperback and eBook)

'Down to Earth' A Fighter Pilot's Experiences of surviving Dunkirk, the Battle of Britain, Dieppe and D-Day. (Grub Street Publishing. 2007)

Author's Website. www.owenzupp.com

www.doitlikeapilot.com

This book is dedicated to the frontline medical staff of the Covid-19 pandemic.

Table Of Contents

Preface 1
Introduction 7
About This Book 9

PART ONE: TECHNIQUES, TACTICS AND STRATEGIES

Introduction: Techniques, Tactics And Strategy 12
Communication: Clarity In Communication 14
Communication: Briefing And Debriefing 18
Communication: Handing Over - Taking Over 22
Communication: Well Chosen Words 24
Communication: Managing Upwards 27
Communication: The Sterile Cockpit 31
Process: The Pilot's Pre-Mortem 33
Process: Power Of The Pause 39
Process: SOPs. Creating An Expectation 44
Process: Organisational Accidents 46
Process: Planning 50
Process: Just Culture 53

Process: Decision Making...57

Process: Check And Training..61

Process: Warning Signs..66

Process: Rejected Take-Offs And Unstable Approaches 70

Process: Finding The Gaps 75

Process: Creating A Diversion 79

People: Much More Than Pilots 83

People: What Is Command?..87

People: Why Good Co-Pilots Can Make Great Captains 95

People: Put Your Oxygen On First..99

People: Check Your Ego 103

People: Check Your Emotions 106

People: CRM. Crew Resource Management 109

People: Cockpit Gradient...113

People: Teamwork...116

People: Making Mistakes..121

People: Groundhog Day..124

People: The Danger Of Distractions..127

People: Situational Awareness - And When You Lose It 132

People: Task Fixation, Saturation And Load Shedding 136

People: Roles, Responsibilities And Trust....................................139

People: The Final Filter...142

Summary Of Techniques, Tactics And Strategy 145

PART TWO THE FRAMEWORK

Introduction: The "Do It Like A Pilot" Framework 154
Framework: Identify Verify Rectify 155
Framework: P.A.I.R. Plan – Advise – Initiate – Review & Report ... 160
Framework: The "Do It Like A Pilot" Framework 164
    One Last Word 171
    About The Author 172
    Acknowledgements 174

Preface

All is right with the world. In a few hours, the sun will be rising, and soon after that, the tyres of the airliner will be touching down in San Francisco. It's been a long night, and the two pilots have all but run out of conversation. They had only met the morning of the flight, but now they both know the basic details of the other. Mike, the captain, had spent his formative years flying fighters in the military. Married young, two full-grown kids at university and a small boat that he never finds time to sail. In the other seat, Sarah is only a little older than Mike's children. She had trained as a cadet pilot with the airline, and having a family is the furthest thing from her mind.

Beyond their shared career in aviation, the two have little in common and yet they are at the helm of the jet as it crosses the ocean with hundreds of passengers trustingly asleep in the darkened cabin. An airline career has been jokingly described as hours of boredom interrupted by moments of sheer terror. While an exaggeration on both counts, the surge of adrenalin that now rushed through Mike and Sarah at that moment offered some validation to the phrase.

The fire handle overhead burst into brilliant red as the bells began ringing simultaneously on the flight deck. From a relaxed posture, both sat up straight and at the ready for their pre-defined roles that were soon to be executed.

"I have control", Mike confirmed, scanning the flight instruments to ensure that first and foremost, the aircraft was flying safely. It was.

He silenced the ringing bells and took a breath, pausing for a moment. That one simple act allowed the "startle factor" to subside and the logical pathways in the brain to resume control over the emotional. "Identify the problem", Mike followed up.

Sarah, equally calmly, methodically scanned the illuminated fire handle for the number printed on its surface and the engine instruments to confirm the problem. The dials agreed with the fire handle; something was wrong with engine number two.

"Engine fire number 2," Sarah stated without an ounce of panic.

Mike balanced his attention between flying the aircraft and verifying what Sarah had just told him. "Number 2 is confirmed. Commence the 'Engine Fire, Severe Damage or Separation' checklist."

From memory, Sarah spoke with an unrushed cadence, and Mike responded in kind.

"Number 2 thrust lever…."

Another pause from Mike, and then, "Confirmed."

"…closed." Sarah slowly retarded the lever to the idle setting for the engine. The aircraft began to slew slightly in the direction of the troubled engine as the asymmetric forces took hold. Mike squeezed in pressure through one of the rudder pedals, keeping the aircraft straight and in balance.

"Number 2 fuel control switch…" Sarah's hand relaxed but at the ready.

Another pause, "Confirmed."

"…Cut-Off." Sarah lowered the corresponding lever, stopping fuel from flowing into the burning engine.

"Number 2 Engine Fire Switch…" Sarah reached towards but again did not action the glowing red handle.

A slightly longer pause for this action was irreversible. It would isolate the engine from a range of other aircraft systems.

"Confirmed."

"…pulled." Sarah pulled the handle from its normal position, although it remained illuminated. "If the Engine Fire Switch remains illuminated…" she looked at Mike.

"It has." He confirmed.

"Rotate the handle to the stop and hold for one second." Sarah put her words into action and in doing so, fired a bottle of extinguishant into the engine.

On the panel an amber, "Bottle Discharged" message illuminated, reassuring them both that she had been successful and cueing Mike to lean forward and start a clock.

After a short time, Sarah spoke with a questioning tone.

"If after 30 seconds, the Engine Fire Switch remains illuminated…"

Mike and Sarah looked at the switch, then at each other and then mutually confirmed that the light had gone out, confirming that the foam injected into the engine had put out the fire. Still, they had a second bottle of extinguishant available if the first had not done the job.

The subsequent flight with an engine shut down will involve a series of calculations, communications and decisions that the crew will prioritise and accomplish. However, even at this early stage, the fact remains that two virtual strangers had combined in harmony to dismiss a significant threat to the safety of their passengers.

And it had taken them less than two minutes.

Fortunately, an engine fire is a rare occurrence, but the smooth co-ordination of flight crews and the safe conveyance of passengers is commonplace - and it is achieved with a success rate in advance of 99.99%. In this era of heightened security and bulletproof flight deck doors, there has never been more mystery surrounding pilots, what they do and how they do it.

Very simply expressed, it is achieved through pre-defined processes, implemented with emotional intelligence that has been learned through training and encouraged through the airline's culture.

Aviation is by its nature a dynamic environment at the mercy of all manner of variables, from engineering issues with an aircraft to the ever-changing weather. Consequently, even the most rigid procedures must be reviewed and implemented with a degree of flexibility, as there is no single checklist that can cover every scenario. And so, it is in our business and personal lives as well. We need a framework to guide us but appreciating the "human factor" is critical in appropriately implementing any plan, strategy or response.

Aviation has not just stumbled upon this methodology; it has continually evolved since the first frail machines took flight. Each time a technological advance was made, whether it be a jet engine or an automatic pilot, the human interface was called upon to adapt. In decades past, mistakes were undoubtedly made, but the industry learned each time before it advanced.

Terms such as Crew Resource Management (CRM), Situational Awareness (SA), "support language", "shared mental model", "cockpit gradient", and "managing upwards" became far more than catchphrases, they became the way goals were achieved with a near-100 per cent success rate. These concepts, which are commonplace in the world of aviation, are equally applicable in the rest of our lives. The purpose of this book is to share a straightforward and actionable means to bring them down from the clouds and into our everyday.

When Captain Chesley "Sully" Sullenberger successfully landed his Airbus airliner on the Hudson River, he had 208 seconds between his engines being rendered useless by the geese they had ingested until the aircraft touched down on the water. It was the first time flying with his co-pilot, First Officer Jeff Skiles, who had only recently completed training on the Airbus A320, and the emergency took place less than five minutes after take-off. Yet, as a crew, they were able to successfully communicate, devise and execute a plan for which there had been no specific training. Furthermore, pilots are trained to recognise the adrenalin rush of being startled in an emergency, that initial period when our body reacts with a fight or flight instinct, and our brain is left to catch up. Panic and anxiety are subdued. Imagine being able to be that effective in less critical situations.

This book opens the flight deck door to describe the techniques, tactics and strategies to allow *you* to do it like a pilot.

Introduction

Every journey begins with the destination.

As a pilot, the primary task is to convey the passengers safely to where they want to go. To achieve this, the weather, facilities, air traffic and a range of other considerations at the destination come into play before the crew ever board the aircraft. Aside from the "Point A to Point B" journey, various contingencies have to be considered and catered for. Simply put, it's how aviators do business. They mitigate risk and implement processes to achieve a safe operation, set to rigorous time constraints in a dynamic environment.

And yet, the very same processes can be implemented in our day to day at ground level. We just rarely do, unless we have been told how.

As a business, a team or as an individual, we have our goals. We seek to guard against failure and provide options should our journey or our goal strike unforeseen problems. The 2020 Covid-19 pandemic is an extreme example of the obstacles that life can throw at us, but it has also reminded us of the importance of having strategies to cope and, ideally, a "Plan B". Or as pilots call it – an alternate airport.

In 2018, the International Air Transport Association (IATA) reported that "4.3 billion passengers flew safely on 46.1 million flights." In doing so, the airlines worldwide achieved a success rate in terms of safety of well beyond 99.99%. Or as IATA's Director General and CEO expressed it, *"...a passenger could take a flight every day for 241 years before experiencing an accident with one fatality on board."*

Contrary to what one might expect, the strategies and tactics employed by air crews to achieve their high levels of success are not complicated. It would be counter-productive in an aircraft that is speeding through the upper atmosphere to require overly involved processes. The environment is continually changing, the resources at hand are limited, and the time available is finite.

Consistency, clarity and conciseness are key elements, and they are equally relevant in the board room, the home or at 38,000 feet. This book seeks to open the flight deck door, dispel the veil of mystery and make these skills your own.

About This Book

On flight decks around the world, the Quick Reference Handbook, or "QRH", sits at the ready. Stowed by a pilot's shin or in a recess by their thigh, it is a core piece of equipment – even in this digital age. As the name infers, it is a concise text to be referred to when needed and with a minimum of fuss. While pilots may not read it cover-to-cover consistently, they frequently plunge into the section of relevance to follow a procedure or rectify an issue when the situation has diverged from normal operations. And so is the case with this book, "Do it like a Pilot".

Each day, millions of people across the world put their lives in the hands of total strangers to safely transport them in a hostile environment at speeds approaching the sound barrier. For those passengers, to do so is an incredible act of trust, bordering upon a leap of faith. In reality, many of the skills, mindsets and processes employed by flight crews are readily transferable into our businesses and even our personal lives.

In the first part of this book, we will investigate a range of tactics and strategies employed by pilots to deal with issues arising from causes as varied as the weather to dealing with each other. Managing people, processes, culture and communications are central to success on the flight deck, just as they are in any business. However, the confined dimensions of the cockpit and the time-critical nature of flight operations mean that the techniques that have evolved are to-the-point and straightforward to implement.

"***Identify - Verify - Rectify***" is a simple, three-word saying that makes perfect sense to any pilot and yet it remains a virtual mystery outside of the cockpit. The second part of this book incorporates this process into a framework, that can be overlaid onto any business to identify, verify and rectify issues in both day-to-day operations, as well as when things have gone off track. Other simple structures in part two are designed to aid in planning, decision-making and "review and report".

In part, the success of flight crews can be attributed to clarity, simplicity and process. This involves taking what may seem to be involved and overwhelming, or even life-threatening, tasks and breaking them down into smaller, logical and achievable steps. This is aided by ongoing training, simple checklists and a culture that emphasises honest, open communication.

This book will explain these methods and offer a framework that can be overlaid upon your business, or your life. Simple and concise. This is *your* QRH.

PART ONE

Techniques, Tactics And Strategies

INTRODUCTION

Techniques, Tactics And Strategy

This first part of the book will reveal and explain a range of techniques, tactics and strategies used by crews to address the issues they encounter, both anticipated and unforeseen. Throughout, the key is to do so effectively and in a timely manner. The flight deck is not the place for conflict and pilots cannot retreat to another office to blow off steam and complain to a colleague. Egos need to be checked, issues addressed, and outcomes reached with a minimum of fuss. As an industry, aviation has evolved to do this with great success, and the methods can be applied universally, even if they are not commonly known outside the industry.

Described simply, tactics address the short-term issue with a specific goal. Strategy is the longer-term planning. Technique is how we can execute these. In airline operations, flight crews are tactical in planning an arrival at their destination, while the airline is strategic in improving overall efficiency. In both cases, a variety of techniques can be employed on a micro-level by the individual and a macro level by the organisation to achieve the result.

As an organisation, airlines and their management play a vital role as a company's culture starts at the top as an element of their overall strategy. From here, the emphasis on safety and efficiency may be generated before the flight operations department devises a range of tactics, under a regulatory framework. The flight crew then operate the aircraft in accordance with these tactics, utilising their techniques, that fall within the regulations, to counter the day-to-day variables.

A point of confusion that can arise is when a technique is conveyed as a procedure. There may be almost limitless techniques to implement a tactic or strategy, while a procedure is a strictly defined method. Managers and leaders can, at times, perceive their technique as the procedure, enforcing their restricted viewpoint upon their subordinate. Pilots can encounter this on check flights and in simulator exercises, and it can be frustrating. Furthermore, in any organisation, this confusion can stifle feedback and the discovery of another, and possibly better, technique. This book will focus on the technique.

For ease of reference, the techniques, tactics and strategies herein have been listed under "People", "Communications", or "Process", even though they may fall under more than one category. The concept of a sound and just "culture" will be covered first as it holds an overarching position on all that will be discussed within this book and is pivotal in implementation and success.

Captains, co-pilots, cabin managers and flight attendants work as successful small teams in the stratosphere every day to safely convey millions of passengers. Here are the techniques, tactics and strategies that make that happen.

COMMUNICATION

Clarity In Communication

To many, hearing aviation jargon, it is a foreign language. In some ways, it may well be. However, it is not the words but the delivery that can make the greatest difference in terms of communication. In an environment filled with background noise and a queue of people waiting to speak on the radio, clarity and conciseness are the essential qualities. And they are qualities that can prove beneficial equally in a radio transmission as it can in a one-on-one discussion at ground level.

Aviation's radio procedures are peculiar to the field as a necessity. Instructions and information must be conveyed quickly at times and without error as a left turn rather than a right turn can have significant ramifications. For six thousand feet not to be confused with sixteen thousand feet, the latter is described as "one-six thousand".

Aviation has its own vocabulary, but in addition to its need for clear, simple communication, it relies on readbacks to verify that the message has not merely been transmitted correctly but read and understood. If any doubt exists, the phrase, "say again" calls for the message to be repeated.

Outside of the flight deck, efficient communication is equally vital to an organisation. It seems that every staff training day has an element of communication skills featured and that poor communication is often cited as a cause of organisational shortcomings. In a world where we have instantaneous communications through phones, texts, emails and all manner of devices, the ability to exchange information correctly still provides a constant challenge. Fortunately, aviation has solved many of the issues, although it is an ongoing process founded on previous history with notable errors.

The world's worst airline accident occurred in 1977 at Tenerife when a take-off clearance was misheard by the captain, compounded by miscommunication within the crew and a reluctance to challenge the captain. The collision of the two 747s killed over 300 people. The ambiguity of phrases such as "Take-Off Power" which, in the heat of the moment, could be interpreted as either setting the power to a take-off setting or removing power altogether – taking it off. The language of aviation needs to be specific, but it is also vital in business.

Communication issues can arise when the words come out at a rapid-fire pace. Unfortunately, it is a common trait that when under pressure, real or perceived, we are prone to speaking too quickly. Think of that presentation that was timed to perfection in rehearsal but was over way too soon when presented to an audience. This tendency is considered in pilot training and countered with the first step being to stop and breathe—the power of the pause. Speech is then given a steady pace – a *cadence* – minimising the need to be repeated.

The *language* used can also be of importance, particularly when the word has dual meanings and needs context. Cadence assists this also in allowing the selection of the most appropriate words to convey the meaning, free of ambiguity. The use of unnecessary words can also hamper efficient communications. Either using additional words, or those that require a dictionary can undermine the message and serve to distract.

Efficient communication is achieved by presenting the information with a minimum of words, a maximum level of clarity and giving equal respect to listening. Not speaking over another and carefully processing their message saves repetition in addition to being polite. It can also aid significantly in formulating your next response.

Considering the *audience* is also appropriate. In an organisation, this is not necessarily limited to their age group, level of education or language skills. Importantly, the message communicated may need to recognise what is important to the audience and that it can vary with the situation. In uncertain times, such as during the days of Covid-19, employees concerns often focused on issues of security – their safety in the workplace and the stability of their workforce. Talk of profits and dividends may strike a hollow note, and even though the profitability may ultimately meet their concerns, the message needs to be expressed directly and in terms that the audience will appreciate.

Confirming that the message is *received* correctly is vital. Misinformation can be as damaging as an absence of information. As mentioned, being respectful and listening is crucial for both parties. Certain situations will call for the information to be read back. Avoid questions that can be answered with a simple, "Yes". For example, rather than asking, "Are you happy with that fuel order?", ask, "How much fuel would you order?" The second question is far more collaborative and less prone to blind obedience, or disinterest.

Cadence – Language – Efficient – Audience – Received. Communication needs to be **CLEAR**.

An organisation's culture and leaders have a significant role to play in effective communication. As stated repeatedly throughout this book, providing the environment for all parties to raise concerns and provide honest feedback without fear of retribution or ridicule, regardless of their standing in the organisation, is not only healthy but valuable. It is a culture that flows from the top down and needs to be reinforced by company policy and personal sincerity.

Communication will undoubtedly continue to be a challenge for organisations of all sizes. However, by recognising that less can mean more and that listening and providing feedback is just as important as being heard, perhaps the message will be CLEAR.

COMMUNICATION

Briefing And Debriefing

In part, aviation achieves its excellent safety record through clarity. A lack of ambiguity in communications and a thorough understanding by all involved. Just as standard operating procedures create an expectation, so too can a standard format when sharing information. The briefing is an essential aspect of this transfer in aviation, and as the name suggests, it is brief – concise. Briefings are not boardroom meetings - they are the short discussion to reinforce the decisions of the boardroom before those plans are executed. And to consider them after the event in the case of a debrief.

Clarity and conciseness are important in this day and age where we find ourselves bombarded by information and distractions. Attention spans are ever-reducing, and if a briefing begins to take on epic proportions, it will become ineffective. In briefing, a level of previous knowledge is accepted, and only the core points need to be revisited in addition to the core threats.

BRIEFING.

Interactive. A briefing is not a lecture. It encourages and requires all participants to be in tune with the content and feel comfortable to provide feedback. Firstly, ensure that you have the team's attention. A technique is to begin with a simple question relating to the plan directed at an individual. This will have everyone tune in just in case they are next. This must be limited to a simple question that is easily answered, or the opportunity to wander off down an irrelevant path may result.

Threats and Considerations. At an early stage, revisit any threats or considerations that were discovered in the "pre-mortem" and planning process and what mitigating strategies have been employed to counter them. This is also an opportunity for the team to raise any concerns that have arisen since the original plan was formulated, or which may occur on the day.

Overview. Revisit the key points in a logical order and reinforce any specific roles and responsibilities that have been assigned.

Contingencies. Reidentify the variables that may occur, necessitating an alternate plan. Define the triggers for these secondary plans and how they will be implemented. Additionally, if a point has been identified at which to abandon the plan, verify that all parties are aware of this. The end of a briefing can be signaled with a final request for suggestions or questions.

In an aviation context, before departure, a briefing would begin with ensuring that everyone is paying attention and a targeted question being asked, possibly about the airport chart. Then, typically threats such as weather or terrain would be considered, and any strategies being used would be reinforced. The departure plan would be reviewed, and finally, the contingencies would be discussed in the case of rejecting the take-off, or at which point it would be continued should an engine fail. The subsequently modified plan would then be highlighted. Any questions? The entire process generally takes five minutes, for, beyond that, distractions may begin to surface.

Briefs can be reduced even further in size and used at any time to confirm that a "shared mental model" exists by all relevant parties and they all have the same appreciation and expectations of the way ahead. Often called "mini-briefs" they are an excellent means of reinforcing Situational Awareness, or SA.

In more urgent situations, where time is a critical element, the format of the "NITS Brief" can convey core information in an accepted form, quickly. Discussed separately in this book, a NITS brief ensures interactivity through requiring a "readback" of the relevant points.

DEBRIEFING.

A valued process in aviation is debriefing, and like the briefing, it can vary in its length dependent upon such elements the depth of the topic being reviewed, or even the time available. It requires similar qualities to a briefing in that it must be interactive, relevant, timely, logical and review any threats, considerations or contingencies that took place. It is an opportunity to recognise and reinforce positive aspects of execution and to review any shortfalls for future learning.

A crew may discuss a departure once they have settled the aircraft in the cruise stage of flight and the debrief may be simply to positively reinforce that it was flown as planned. It may be to highlight an anomaly with Air Traffic Control or a better technique to manage the flight path.

A longer debrief will take place after each flight to review the process. After an emergency or abnormal situation, a captain will gather the entire flight deck and cabin crews to operationally debrief the event and to check on their welfare.

When a debrief does recall a shortfall in some aspect, its identification is for future improvement. If the crew has made an error or failed in some part of the operation, then the first step is for the captain, as the leader, to share ownership of the shortfall. This will put the crew at ease, and the humility exhibited by the captain will encourage open discussion and therein lies the key to learning.

If an individual within the crew has made an error, the focus remains on the error and improvement, not the individual. The adage to "praise in public and criticise in private" is to be respected. And within that criticism, there is still a technique to ensure morale is not eroded. Sometimes called a "crap sandwich", the debriefing of a team or individual after an incident is best handled by commencing with the positives, then addressing the shortfall. Beginning with a negative will potentially dishearten and the valid points not finding their mark. Finishing with a positive aspect of the operation and checking on welfare concludes the debrief with the crew feeling upbeat and valued.

A debrief can be succinctly explained as a means to review, report and respond. Accordingly, an organisation must have a culture, training and process in place to facilitate this.

Debriefs are timely, immediately after the event, regardless of success or failure and will define any responses or reports that may be required by issues, both good and bad, that have been discovered. They do not seek to assign blame in a just culture; they seek improvement and are one of the most valuable learning tools available as they are based upon real-life execution and not a perceived plan.

Briefings can mitigate against threats in advance while debriefs can provide incredible value through considering the execution in retrospect. The open, honest, and focused discussion immediately before and after the implementation of a plan is simply a part of airline culture. It is a technique that many pilots carry into their personal lives and is undoubtedly a technique that can benefit any organisation.

COMMUNICATION

Handing Over – Taking Over

In reading some old-World War Two flight training accident reports, there was an incredible common cause attributed to several landing accidents involving the old biplanes. It was incredible because each pilot thought the other was flying and as a result, the aircraft "landed" itself with no-one at the controls.

It sounds ridiculous, but there were several contributing factors. Firstly, the student sat in front of the instructor in a remote cockpit of their own. Communication was through a Gosport Tube, a simple system of tubing that joined a fixed mouthpiece in the instructor's cockpit to the earpieces inside the student's leather helmet – and vice versa. Instructions would be yelled down the tube to the student in competition with the noise coming from the nearby engine and the rushing airflow, for these were the days of open cockpits and flying goggles, with no enclosure.

Traditionally, there has been a tactile act nicknamed shake and take where one pilot jiggles the control column to hand over, and the other jiggles it in reply to confirm that they have taken over control. It is still done where pilots sit one behind the other, while flight decks side-by-side seating rely on verbal confirmation. Generally, "Handing Over" and "Taking Over". Regardless of the technique, the imperative is that it is always clear who has control of the aircraft.

Even when safely on the ground, flight crews will often hand their aircraft over to another crew. It is accompanied by a simple brief of the aircraft's status, including any maintenance issues being attended to and possibly what the weather was like inbound to assist the outbound crew's planning for departure. Reports of turbulence may require that the "Fasten Seat Belts" sign remains illuminated longer after take-off, a piece of information that is useful to both cabin crew and passengers.

The simple process of "handing over" is clear and concise. It dispels ambiguity and allows one party to focus on a task while freeing the other to move on. The language need not be as restrictive as on a flight deck, however, having a universally recognised "trigger" within an organisation adds a great deal of clarity to identify who has a specific responsibility at any given time. Ensuring that roles and duties are positively accounted for is equally applicable in the course of a workday, or the case of an employee taking leave. It can be frustrating when a task is left uncompleted, or a deadline is missed, and the only rebuttal is, "I thought that you were doing it." In an aircraft, the consequences can be even greater.

In some instances, the transfer of responsibility may need to be documented, and at other times this may not be required. However, in addition to establishing who has "command" a written or verbal briefing is always advisable to allow the new pilot of the project to move forward with momentum. Additionally, it provides an opportunity to raise questions. A pilot doesn't generally leave the flight deck immediately after they have handed over control, so they are still available to provide supporting information if that need subsequently becomes apparent.

It is a simple procedure used by pilots around the world, but with that simplicity comes safety and clarity. Positively ensuring that responsibility for a task has been handed over enhances efficiency through one party commencing from an informed standpoint and the other free to deploy their efforts elsewhere. Don't ever be left wondering who's landing the aircraft.

COMMUNICATION

WELL CHOSEN WORDS

It came to be known as the "Miracle on the Hudson.". Less than three minutes after Sully's Airbus A320 encountered a flock of geese, the aircraft was touching down on the waters of the Hudson River. Even so, as the captain, Sullenberger managed to get a brief announcement out to the passengers and crew, warning them to "brace for impact". It was an order that the flight attendants repeated and reinforced until the aircraft came to a halt.

Although an extreme case, this emphasises the importance of clear and concise communications, particularly when events diverge from the norm. As stress further impedes our ability to communicate effectively, many airlines adopt a formal structure to relay vital information that is both brief and unambiguous. Known as the "**NITS** Brief", the format is easily applied to all manner of communications.

NITS stands for the *Nature of the problem – Intentions - Time Available - Special Instructions.*

For example, in the event of an engine failure, a NITS Briefing to the senior flight attendant would typically be, "The nature of the problem is that we have a technical issue which has resulted in us shutting down one of our engines. We are safe, and the aircraft is flying normally. Our intention is to divert to Los Angeles. We will be landing in one hour. There are no special instructions, and we anticipate a normal landing."

Importantly, the cabin crew member will then be asked to read the information back to confirm that all details are correct. As such, the crew will often write the details down. This is a critical step as there is no room for misinterpretation, particularly as the senior cabin crew member will then be responsible for briefing the rest of the crew.

The NITS structure is also ideal when the time comes for the Captain to announce the critical incident to the passengers through the public address, or PA, system. There will be "softer" edges to the wording for the passengers, but the NITS format provides everything the passengers need to know. The "Special Instructions" can be as general as, "Always follow your crew members' instructions."

Beyond aviation, NITS is an ideal means to gather thoughts and concisely convey a message, whether or not time is a critical factor. Furthermore, whether writing an email, a memo, or speaking to a room full of employees, the format is simple yet informative. Even when the required description is to be more expansive, NITS is an excellent starting point for providing the initial structure around which the finer details can be built. An introduction and a conclusion may also be added, but at the core, NITS provides the substance in a logical order.

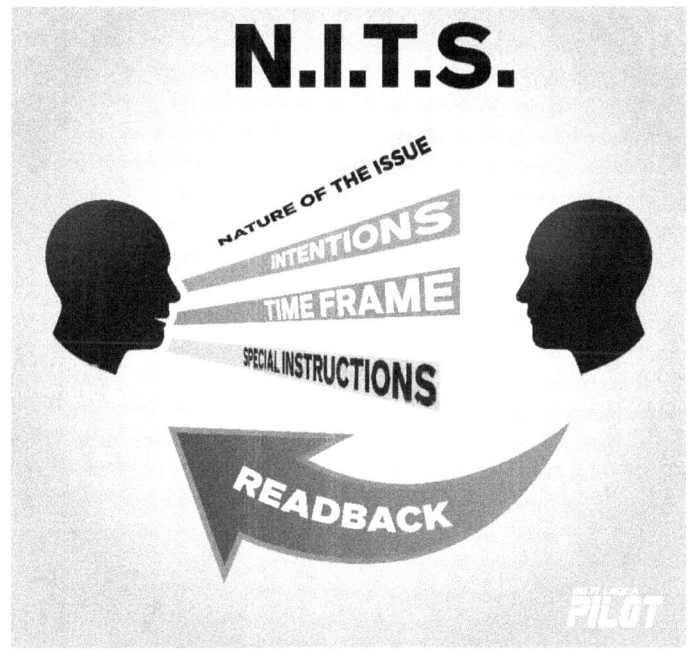

The phrasing that supports NITS may be modified for general use to remove the overtones of an emergency. It may be an "issue" rather than a "problem", and rather than time being a limiting factor, a broader application can be described as a "Timeframe". Hence, the "modified NITS" can be rewritten as;

N - **N**ature of the issue.
I - **I**ntentions.
T - **T**imeframe.
S - **S**pecial Instructions.

NITS may be born of urgent demand, but the truth is that it is one of the most adaptable forms of concise communication to crew, family and workers alike. Rather than staring at a blinking cursor wondering where to begin that memo, write down NITS and go from there with clarity and efficiency.

COMMUNICATION

Managing Upwards

In the chapter, "Check Your Ego", we examined how the bristling personality trait can impede communication and other processes to the overall detriment of the greater good and the completion of the task. From domineering captains to passive-aggressive co-pilots, there is no room in the confines of the flight deck for a dysfunctional crew. However, even when harmony exists, there can still be a power gradient, perceived or real, that can deter a co-pilot from speaking up. Even when a captain or manager has created an environment where feedback and open communication is encouraged, it can prove difficult for some subordinates to do so without worrying about causing offence or worrying that they are wrong. To this end, the technique of "managing upwards" has become commonplace – in fact, even a staged process has been designed.

In effect, managing upwards calls for a junior employee to "manage the manager" and consequently, the technique can work for leaders as well. The critical element is to use emotional intelligence to raise the issue in a non-confrontational way so that tensions aren't raised, and communication hampered moving forward. You are speaking up because you **C.A.I.R.**

C – Convey Information.

A – Ask the question. "Do you know that we…?", "Are we going to…?"

I – "I" Statement. "I'm concerned …", "I'm not confident …", I'm not comfortable …"

R – Offer a Resolution. "Perhaps we could…", "Another option would be to…"

Let's look at each point individually.

C. Convey Information. In the first instance, it is essential to convey the information that is relevant without necessarily any personal attachment. Basically, a statement of fact that might trigger a recollection. This can be phrased, "We are…" in order to accept and share ownership of the situation.

A. Ask the question. Asking a relevant question calls for a response and is one stage advanced beyond making a statement while retaining the "we" element. However, they still may simply state "Yes" or "No", which does not indicate an understanding of the situation. If nothing changes, then further action needs to be taken.

I. "I Statement". Emotional intelligence and a subdued ego now come into play. Heightening your concern to reach out to the other party by expressing your personal level of discomfort.

R. Resolution. The captain or manager may still be unable to perceive the issue or may just be having a bad day. Suggesting a resolution or a plan, can relieve the pressure valve and offer an alternative course of action. It doesn't matter who suggests it – the priority is always the safe and efficient execution of the task.

On the flight deck, there is also a further and final step. Due to the nature of flight, if there is still no action being taken, diplomacy is dispensed with, and a straightforward approach is initiated. The language may begin with a direct instruction, such as "You must…!", or in an extreme case, the other pilot takes over control of the aircraft. It is worth emphasising that these instances are rare and merely conveying the relevant information will usually produce the desired result.

An airborne example could be that a co-pilot is concerned that the captain is not slowing the aircraft down adequately to prepare for a landing.

C – Convey Information. "We are still doing 300 knots."

A – Ask the Question. "Do you know that we have to be at 210 knots by ten miles from the airport?"

I – I Statement. "I'm concerned that we are not slowing down and will be too fast for the approach to land."

R- Resolution. "Would you like me to extend the landing gear now to help us to slow down?"

From this example, you can see that another escalation may be needed in an aviation sense if these four stages have not produced a satisfactory response.

A more mundane example could be an overlooked power bill, with the reminder threatening to cut the power to the business premises.

C - Convey Information. "This power bill is high this quarter. It's $750."

A - Ask the Question. "Do you know that the bill was due last month?"

I - I Statement. "I'm concerned that if we don't pay this bill now, they might cut off the power."

R - Resolution. "Would you like me to call the power company to pay the bill?

This example is simplistic, displaying that it is equally available to a speeding jet and an overdue bill. It is non-offensive, thus avoiding a clash of personalities. It is staged, so the concern is raised in a measured fashion. It closes with the offering of a solution.

In some cases, particularly if the timeframe is critical, the employee can step into the process at any stage as they see fit. These are instances when the urgency of the task and the severity of the consequences call for an expedited process with less "diplomacy".

If managing upwards and the C.A.I.R language can be merged into the company culture, it becomes even more effective. The phrasing and the sequence will most likely trigger an immediate recognition that the other party is raising concern. The earlier in the sequence that a solution is reached, the level of impact and possible embarrassment will be lessened.

Furthermore, when a manager recognises that they have been "managed", it's an ideal opportunity to check in the ego, recognise the fact and thank the employee or junior manager. It displays humility, leadership and encourages continued vigilance and feedback in the future.

Managing upwards is not a "trick"; it is a technique. Embedded within a company's culture, it is yet another tool in the toolbox to improve efficiency and avoid conflict.

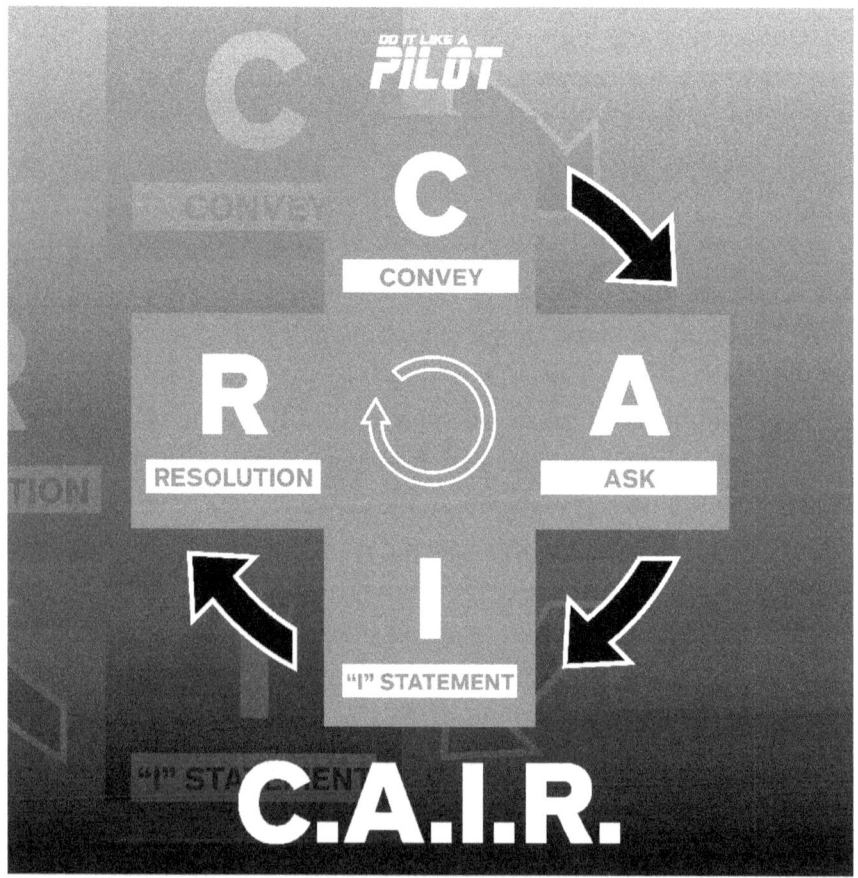

COMMUNICATION

THE STERILE COCKPIT

In 1981, the United States' Federal Aviation Administration (FAA) introduced the "Sterile Cockpit Rule". As with so many aviation rules and regulations, it had been born of tragedy. Some years before, an airliner had been on its approach to land, one of the most critical phases of flight. Readying the aircraft to land calls to reconfigure the aircraft's flaps and landing gear, as well as flying a specific approach path while descending ever closer to the terrain. In the aftermath of the accident, the Cockpit Voice Recorder (CVR) revealed that the crew were involved in non-operational, unrelated conversation that detracted from the safe operation of the aircraft throughout the approach. There were few survivors when the jet impacted the terrain.

In the interceding years, the Sterile Cockpit Rule has become commonplace within airlines around the world, with each company defining their parameters. Many call for the pilots to limit their conversation to operational issues below 20,000 feet, both on departure and arrival. Furthermore, they establish "No Contact" periods when the cabin crew cannot contact the flight deck, to guard against distracting the flight crew at critical times. Typically, these may be from the engines "spooling up" on take-off until the wheels are retracted. Then, on the approach to land, from the wheels being extended until the landing roll has been completed. In the broader Sterile Cockpit periods, cabin crew should only contact the pilots for urgent operational issues.

In aviation, distracting conversations can have safety implications and still, the sterile cockpit has a place in the business world. All too often, meetings and professional discussions can wander off-topic. The effect is that the primary task is ignored to its detriment, and inevitably valuable time is wasted. Additionally, some parties will become disengaged and should the meeting return to its purpose; their attention may have already been lost.

There is a time and place for free thought and discussion on broader issues, and meetings can be organised for this purpose. Still, when a specific project is nominated for consideration, such meetings should be marked accordingly. The meeting's agenda can be annotated as a "Sterile Cockpit" meeting to remind participants of the significance and the focus needed on the topic. It is also an invitation to attendees to call out any conversation that is wandering away from the central purpose. Even the conference room door can be marked, "Sterile Cockpit", to advise co-workers of the focused meeting taking place.

However, bear in mind, that just as airline operations allow the cabin crew to make contact with the pilots in the case of a greater operational need, fellow workers should be made aware that they can interrupt proceedings, but only if a significant event dictates this happens.

Focus and time-critical challenges are not limited to the domain of aviation. All business can benefit from targeted dialogue and the time savings that will inevitably result.

PROCESS

✈

THE PILOT'S PRE-MORTEM

The purpose of a post-mortem is well understood. Through careful examination, the coroner is seeking to confirm the cause of death. In some cases, the individuals were the victims of fatal car accidents or heart attacks that had taken their lives all too soon. Through the meticulous process of examining the workings of a human body in detail, we better understand anatomy and therefore, potentially provide better treatment to future patients.

Unfortunately, a post-mortem is precisely that – after death. For that patient, the lessons to be learned from their passing were of no benefit to them. The damage had already been done. Even so, pilots and organisations can perform a post-mortem on their operation as an aspect of debriefing. That is to say, that they can dissect the operation to see which element was the shortfall and to be guarded against in the future. And what the strengths are to be reinforced and repeated in the future.

Less well-known is the concept of a "pre-mortem", and it is generally attributed to Gary Klein PhD. As a decision-making tool, it seeks to identify failings before they take place, rather than examining them retrospectively. As a technique, the pre-mortem has gained substantial momentum in the business world and with good reason. Costly mistakes can be seen before they arise, and time wasted pursuing fruitless paths can be prevented.

In aviation, the pre-mortem has been a part of daily life for decades, although it has remained fundamentally untitled beyond asking, "What if?". Each time an aircraft takes to the sky, it doesn't merely carry sufficient fuel to fly from one airport to another. It carries additional fuel to cater for a range of variables that could potentially affect the flight – and there are many. The four engines of a fully laden Boeing 747 may be consuming 10 tons of fuel an hour as it waits for a storm to pass to permit its take-off. Enroute, the same jet may sit comfortably at altitude; however, an emergency such as the loss of cabin pressurisation can lead to the oxygen masks dropping from the overhead panels. Critically there is a need for the aircraft to descend rapidly to a level where more oxygen-rich air exists. And a level where the aircraft will burn substantially more fuel.

The seemingly limitless range of variables are all factored into a pilot's pre-mortem, and it is more than merely a flight planning exercise. It is a mindset that is encouraged in air crew from their first flight and trained for time and again in flight simulators. As they are perched in the stratosphere with the autopilot engaged, pilots will routinely check the weather at ports they are not planned to land at and ask, "What if?". What if an engine failed now, where would we go? What if fog forms unexpectedly at our destination, what is our alternate plan? Air crew continually anticipate scenarios that may never occur, but by doing so, they head off any shortcomings and always have a plan prepared. This principle of pre-mortem can be equally and successfully applied to our lives and business.

Elsewhere in this book, we frequently discuss culture – the environment within an organisation that encourages or discourages certain qualities and behaviours. For a pre-mortem to work effectively, the first step is to have a culture that permits its existence, and this can mean breaking away from the norm. Even before the stakeholders gather in the conference room or the living room, the correct culture must be in place.

This means encouraging pessimism in the face of an exciting new prospect and embracing hypothetical scenarios beyond the normal bounds. So often, our mindset can focus on our strengths, but in a pre-mortem, we need to examine our weaknesses closely. The process will counter over-confidence but ultimately bolster genuine confidence once the process is complete.

Most importantly, the culture must encourage people at all levels to speak up and criticise. Too often, such comments can be perceived as dissent, but in a healthy environment, this type of disagreement must be encouraged to avoid a "group think" mentality. Blind following is one of the quickest ways to overlook lurking dangers.

As a crew gather before a flight, they will examine all of the information available to them. Weather briefings and "Notices to Airmen" that outline any issues affecting their route, from unserviceable runways to rumbling volcanoes. As a group, they will discuss the "What ifs?" and how they can mitigate against an undesired event. This may take the form of amending the route, carriage of extra fuel to facilitate various options and additional flight time, or a range of tactics and strategies.

Importantly, all pilots within the crew, regardless of rank, are encouraged to speak up and highlight possible negative scenarios. Frequently, the captain will call upon the most junior pilot to be the first to brief the rest of the crew and raise any issues, further preventing a "group think". This action states from the outset that the captain encourages all input from all parties, independent of any formal hierarchy or rank structure that may exist. Furthermore, when issues are raised, the captain needs to recognise and appreciate the input to reinforce the culture further and encourage others to be open and honest.

In a business environment, the process may be the same, but the questions will differ. What if the marketing plan fails? What if a supplier falls behind schedule? What if revenue is less than projected, or costs are greater? A post-mortem examines the cause of death. A business pre-mortem seeks to prevent that death by identifying hypothetical problems and planning for them in advance. Should they arise, there is a strategy already in place, allowing for proactive rather than reactive measures.

A pre-mortem can even be applied to our personal lives, and again, pessimism must be taken in the correct context, and everyone must have a voice. The goal is to foresee situations against which to safeguard, not to be caught in a web of gloom. Once again, we apply the "What ifs?". What if my employment ceases? What if our house catches fire? What if our home renovation runs over schedule?

Whether in a business or personal setting, anticipating those events that are usually unanticipated allows them to be addressed rationally and in a balanced manner, should they occur. With a pre-mortem completed, the decision-making process can be made well in advance and free from the pressures of time compression and deadlines that may arise at the time. This allows for more available mental capacity and resources to attend to any variations from the forecast issue.

In a basic sense, the workplace already possesses a form of pre-mortem in its building's fire procedures. There are initial actions, assigned roles, evacuation routes and assembly points for headcounts. It is a prepared plan, founded on pessimism for a hypothetical eventuality that hopefully never takes place.

The same principles can apply in planning a pre-mortem for a business project.

1. As discussed, the first step is the biggest – creating a healthy culture. This must be achieved before any meeting takes place and will need time, leadership and ongoing promotion to maintain. With all stakeholders present and encouraged to voice their thoughts, the process can take place.

2. At the commencement of the meeting, outline the project and its goals.
3. Ask the "What ifs?" and allow the group to imagine failure. As each potential weakness is identified, note it down in plain view for all to see and share. It is essential to encourage wide and varied input at this stage, with nothing out of bounds. Also, be aware that some "What ifs?" can give rise to new issues.
4. Assess the risk of each potential failure. Risk is considering the likelihood in conjunction with the consequences. An unlikely event may have terminal consequences so it needs to be addressed, while a minor failing, though likely, may have minimal impact.
5. Prioritise the failings and create a plan in advance to counter them should they occur.
6. Compile the strategies post-meeting and share among the stakeholders.
7. As the project proceeds, periodically revisit the process to confirm that the projected strategies are still relevant and to identify any emerging, "What ifs?"

In the vast majority of cases, a project, or a flight, will proceed without any of the eventualities ever occurring. However, by conducting an effective pre-mortem, potential problems can be identified and guarded against before the aircraft ever takes flight. The result is that the flight will not be unexpectedly exposed to vulnerabilities in the air.

Interestingly, sometimes a strategy cannot initially be found to counter an apparent failure, and this happens in aviation, too. An airliner's fuel tanks can only hold a finite amount of fuel. On occasions, the weather at the destination comes with a significant delay to air traffic or may even prevent flying an approach to land. A new route may need to be flown with an extra port of call to replenish the fuel tanks with enough fuel to cover these contingencies and still have the endurance to fly to another airport. In a business project, an extra step, an additional resource or staffing may be required to bridge the gap.

Even then, there are times when flights are delayed significantly or cancelled in the interests of safety, and so it can be with any project. However, the conduct of a pre-mortem allows this to take place before the project has proceeded too far. It is often said that "It is better to be on the ground wishing that you were in the air than the other way around." And this can be applied to a range of situations.

Pre-mortems call for us to loosen the grip on our optimism and encourage dissent – two uncommon aspects in most settings. However, by asking "What if?" and imagining failure before it is a reality, the chance of ultimate success is significantly increased.

PROCESS

Power Of The Pause

It is said that fools rush in where angels fear to tread. The truth is that there are very few situations in life and work that require immediate action, and yet the ramifications of a rushed incorrect choice can be catastrophic.

Have you ever sent an email that you regretted, the second you hit "Send"? Made a purchase purely on impulse? Or said something hurtful to a loved one? The ramifications of that snap decision or ill-considered communication can be long-lasting and in the world of aviation – fatal.

For an air crew, the most critical phase of flight can be the take-off. An engine failing as the aircraft takes to the air leaves the pilots dealing with controlling the aircraft's flight path, both directionally and vertically as it seeks to climb away from the ground safely. Should the engine also be on fire, the situation may be even more urgent as flames trail from the engine, creating a great deal of distress in the passenger cabin. However, on the flight deck, there is no place for panic.

As dire as the situation may seem, the crew must not rush the process. Even when loaded to its capacity, the aircraft can slowly climb away with a failed engine if it is flown correctly. In the cockpit, the pilots are trained to methodically identify the failed engine and confirm that it is the correct engine before they action the procedure to make it safe and secure. This procedure involves shutting the engine down to stop it spinning and potentially causing more damage, vibration or fire. Importantly, none of this takes place until the aircraft achieves a minimum height above the ground. There is an intentional pause.

Often referred to as "sitting on your hands", the pause is to ensure that priorities remain in order and that procedures are executed correctly. First and foremost, to keep the aircraft flying, as the most immediate threat is potentially losing control or flying into the ground. The quickest way for this to happen would be to rush the procedure and shut down the engine that is functioning properly. And it has been done!

Our modern instantaneous society seems to be at odds with the concept of sitting on our hands. Voicemail, texts, email, alarms, search engines and even diets seem to scream for immediate attention, but just as there are bells ringing and flashing lights in the cockpit, in life and business, *we* must dictate the schedule of events.

Our physiology is instinctively triggered by the startle factor – our "fight or flight" reflex. It leads us to react, rather than respond. Our emotional brain overpowers rational thought until the correct chemical balance can be re-established. Pausing allows our body and brain to catch up and behave as we should, not as we feel.

The length of the pause will be dictated by the timeframe and nature of the issue. In conversation, the pause may be momentary, allowing us enough time to gather our thoughts and respond effectively. If the issue is related to a purchase, we may take days to research comparable products. If it is an aircraft engine on fire, the process will need to be conducted promptly after a short pause in which the safe flight path of the aircraft is assured, and the offending engine positively identified and confirmed.

In a face-to-face situation, pausing can be difficult and made increasingly so if tensions are high. Arguments and conflicts tend to have their inertia driven by an emotional reaction. Even so, pausing for just a moment can arrest the rate of decay and calm the air and give the impression of a considered response. Even if only biting one's tongue for a moment is the reality. The pause allows you to take command of the pace and apply your procedures at the pace you dictate.

However, pausing should not be confused with procrastination. In pausing, there is a definite timeframe. It may be six seconds or six days, but at the end of that period, the plan will be executed. Conversely, procrastination is open-ended, drifting on without a framework. And just as ignoring or unnecessarily delaying attending to a failed engine can lead to further damage that is potentially catastrophic, so too can procrastinating over decisions in our life and business. A pause is finite – procrastination is not.

A simple strategy to counter the temptation of rushing in is the mnemonic, **STOP**. A short word for what may be a brief pause that can also be applied to more complex situations.

S – Stop and Breathe.

T – Timeframe.

O – Options

P – Plan and Execute.

Stop for a moment and take a breath. That's the first easy step. If the aircraft is under effective autopilot control, some airlines train pilots to place their hands on their laps initially to avoid an incorrect, rushed input. Whether it is said out loud or used to recognise and harness the startle factor mentally will depend upon the setting. Either way, this single word can bring the focus to what is a matter of priority. Is the aircraft in a safe place with adequate fuel and airspeed? How do I respond to the question that I have just been asked? Should I make this investment? In any situation, stopping reminds us to pause and assess, rather than react. It is also an opportunity to show some humility and ask, "What did I just do? Did I create this event?

Next, we need to consider the *timeframe*. In a conversation, the pause may be just long enough to collect our thoughts. The pause doesn't necessarily have to be a period of silence, with any number of suitable phrases you can make the other party aware that you are thinking through a response. In a business decision, the timeframe may be much greater, but still, the pause must be defined.

With the logical neural pathways taking command over impulse, the situation can be assessed, and a range of *options* considered. Logic can now make the choice, rather than an emotional reaction to perceived limited options.

In the final step, and keeping procrastination at bay, we *plan and execute*. Whether that is a verbal response, a decision to enter a contract or treating a patient in a twisted motor vehicle, we initiate our plan. And as discussed in decision-making, we still need to reassess our plan and execution as it evolves.

A pause may be momentary, but the consequences of acting immediately and on impulse can be terminal. In avoiding being rushed, we operate on our terms and in a timeframe that allows both our physiology and our mental capacity to respond appropriately. At times, it can be difficult. Whether they are the warning bells in a cockpit, the pleads of an injured patient, or the pressures of everyday life, the environment can strongly suggest a deadline that does not genuinely exist. It is up to us to pause and take back command of the situation.

PROCESS

SOPs.
Creating An Expectation

Standard Operating Procedures, or SOPs, are the core structure for flight crew operations and communication. However, while this terminology may suggest that such a term is solely applicable to the strictly disciplined environment of the flight deck, the truth is very different. In fact, SOPs by another name can be a pivotal key to improving any process, anywhere.

SOPs are born out of efficiency but produce enhanced understanding, awareness and even safety. In the first instance, procedures seek to achieve a goal with a minimum of fuss and maximum transparency. In many cases, they may support processes that are to be repeated and highlight the time saved by not re-inventing the wheel. Frequently in aviation, SOPs have originated as the result of a previous incident or accident which demonstrated a flawed approach. Seeking to relearn and repeat unnecessarily is equally important in business as it is on the flight deck.

Specifically, even the words used in a briefing may be standardised. The procedures used to start an aircraft's engines, order fuel or deal with a loss of cabin pressure at altitude are all outlined in the array of manuals with which pilots are familiar.

More broadly, SOPs create a level of expectation through a shared perspective, sometimes known as a "shared mental model". In turn, this expectation flags a divergence from protocol and offers other parties an immediate reference point from which they can identify and raise an omission or shortfall. Beyond efficiency, it is this degree of expectation that is the real strength of SOPs.

Should a pilot inadvertently miss the selection of a switch from "Off" to "On", the other pilot will recognise this deviation from the Standard Operating Procedures and raise the point. In the rare case that it is an intentional deviation from SOPs, that procedure provides an immediate justification to challenge the actions of the other pilot. That being said, there may be a genuine reason to diverge from the procedure in an emergency, but SOPs call for that to be clarified.

In a business situation, less formal SOPs can exist that can prove equally valuable. We have already mentioned the broad framework of "Identify – Verify – Rectify" (IVR) when addressing an issue. If an organisation has a culture that embraces this framework, an expectation is created that following the discovery of a problem, there will be a pause when that problem is positively identified as the core issue. Thus, saving time, effort and resources by avoiding venturing down the incorrect path of rectification.

Should a manager or employee hurriedly rush into initiating a solution without considering, or "verifying", the nature of the problem, the company SOP of "Identify – Verify – Rectify" will raise a red flag to the oversight. Other team members will not only expect that there is a step between identifying a problem and fixing it, but they can readily refer to "IVR" when they raise their concerns.

SOPs offer a shared expectation that allows managers and employees alike to be on the same page with a degree of mutual accountability. As the term suggests, it is a standard way of operating that is understood by everyone within the organisation. SOPs are not complicated, but they do apply to all parties equally, and any divergence is bound to a path of reasoning. Not an apology at a later date.

PROCESS

Organisational Accidents

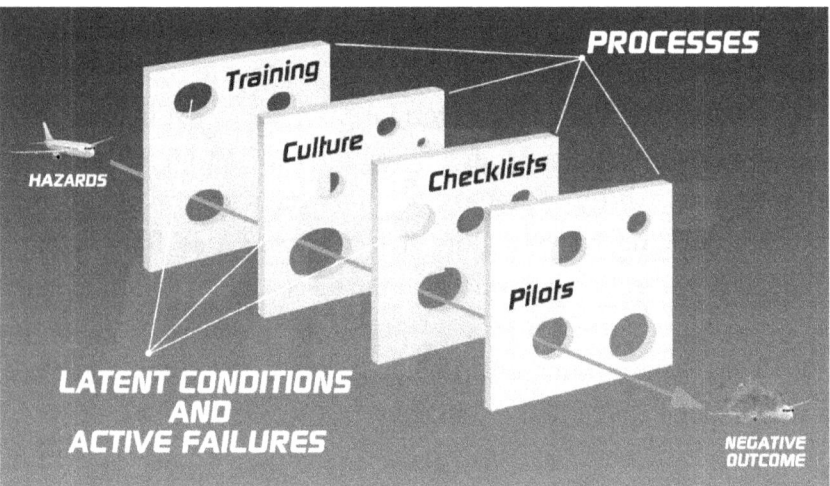

Too often, the symptoms of an accident are readily recognised and addressed, while the real causes are overlooked and left unattended ready to strike again at a future date. This has long been understood in aviation, where once everything was blamed upon "Pilot Error". The problem with this philosophy was that it inferred that if that particular pilot was removed from the equation, then the situation would not happen again. This was obviously incorrect.

On closer examination, an accident was seen to be the culmination of a range of factors leading up to the final event. Some were within the pilot's control, and some they were not even aware of – organisational failings buried deep within the airline's structure or processes.

Air crash investigators came to understand that the path to prevention was to address the range of contributing factors.

The concept was eloquently described by Professor James Reason from the University of Manchester, who created the "Swiss Cheese Model" as a metaphor. In his model, Professor Reason drew a parallel to slices of Swiss Cheese, complete with holes, and each slice representing a point at which an action could have prevented the final outcome. For the aircraft accident to occur, the holes in at least four slices of cheese had to line up. An accident may be prevented simply by a checklist catching an omission, or more deeply rooted, through a company culture that encourages and facilitates open communication by all parties. Frequently, the pilots are the final slices of cheese, the final filter.

To better understand the depth at which causal factors may be embedded, we can look at the Swiss Cheese Model more closely. The "holes" in the cheese are the weaknesses within an organisation through which a project can slip. Latent conditions are those issues buried deeply and may well go unnoticed until it is too late, perhaps an airline possesses a culture of pressuring crews to depart on time, or a failure to update a manual to reflect a change in procedures. By comparison, active failures are acts that have an immediate and negative effect, such as the crew omitting to lower the landing gear before landing or turning contrary to instructions and towards rising terrain.

There may be more than the four examples of causal factors in the diagram, and their nature may be far more wide-ranging. Within an organisation, identifying the various processes that already exist is a starting point before refining the perspective and actively seeking out latent conditions that may exist. Again, culture plays a vital role in discovering potential weaknesses. And there will always be weaknesses.

There is no such thing as a risk-free endeavour, although the operation of an airliner is exceptionally safe. In other cases, it is always a matter of balance. If an airline were to be entirely risk-free, it would ground its aircraft, and that would bankrupt the airline. Even if the airline placed highly restrictive operating parameters on weather restrictions and fuel reserves above and beyond those already in place, it would ultimately become unviable. Conversely, if the airline chose to operate below the minimum safety standards and placed profits wildly over safety, it would quite possibly go bankrupt in the wake of a regulatory grounding, or a catastrophic accident. As James Reason identifies, in a company, the challenge is to maintain a level of moderation and continually evaluate where the company sits between being productive and protected. In most companies, managers may well have a production focus, simply because of the nature of the industry. Still, measures need to be in place to provide a level of protection, also.

While long term strategies such as company culture and training can create a baseline, it may be personnel, standards checks and reporting that identifies a trend away from the median. Such tracking is used effectively in airlines to highlight aspects of the operation that need to be addressed. There may be a spike in non-compliance with an air traffic control clearance, or onboard monitors may detect an increased number of touchdowns beyond the ideal landing zone. Modified training and procedures can be targeted to guard against this trend from drifting away from a safe level of protection. In turn, airlines monitor the carriage of fuel beyond the flight plan recommendation watching if there is a drift away from production. Bearing in mind, the crew have the final responsibility for the carriage of fuel.

Whether a matter of protection or production, an organisation must encourage all staff at all levels to be vigilant and raise concerns. Self-reporting of incidents must not be done under a veil of possible punishment, and a simple reporting system must be in place. Reporting must be recognised, receive feedback and be positively reinforced.

Checklists are another proven measure that airlines have adopted with great success. Gradually, the philosophy of using checklists has been implemented in a broad range of industries, from medicine to mining. A simple, final written check can take moments to complete but guard against a significant error.

In any undertaking, there will always be hazards with potentially negative consequences. Sometimes these hazards will be deep within an organisation and at other times, right at the operational edge. Regardless, defences will need to be put in place between the hazard and the potential loss. That is why James Reason's "Swiss Cheese Model" is both eloquent and relevant to any organisation.

PROCESS

PLANNING

The planning of an airline flight draws input from a broad scope of departments. From commercial to safety, to load control and engineering, meteorological services and many more. For pilots, planning a flight is a routine task, that draws together this expertly gathered information which has been summarised into a flight plan that details the route. Additionally, there is a range of weather reports, charts and pages of information regarding airports, airways, navigation aids, and a list too long to include here. This detail has been provided by others, allowing the crew to focus on the operational aspects.

Armed with the data, the planning process can begin when the crew meet for the briefing before the flight. It is commonplace that the crew will have already considered the information before the crew comes together, thus streamlining the process. The captain will generally lead the briefing but may delegate the task to a subordinate as an exercise in learning. Either way, the environment will be established for all crew members to question openly, suggest, and as appropriate, disagree throughout the planning phase and the entire flight.

Planning structures will vary with each organisation; the following is a typical planning structure for a flight crew that can be easily overlaid onto a range of situations.

GOAL.

In most flight operations, the broad-based goal will be for a safe, on-time arrival at the destination. This will be portrayed in the flight plan.

THREATS AND CONSIDERATIONS.

The crew will consider any potential issues that may affect a standard operation. It may be an engineering issue with the aircraft or weather en route or at the destination. Certain altitudes may have headwinds, and others forecast turbulence. Even the recent experience of the crew on a particular route is considered. Using a "pre-mortem" technique, the issues will be considered with a range of "What if?" scenarios. In turn, the balance of probability and consequence - that is, the level of risk.

RISK MITIGATION.

For those issues presenting a level of risk, a strategy to mitigate against them will be agreed upon. With weather unsuitable at the destination, carrying enough fuel to attempt an arrival and still be able to divert may be a strategy. In extreme cases, such as the presence of a typhoon or volcano, the airline may cancel the service before it departs.

There may be potential issues enroute which will call for consideration. An airport normally available for emergencies may be closed for runway maintenance, or military operations may preclude a direct route. It is essential to consider the task by looking left and right, not just straight ahead, solely focused on the destination.

Whether through the carriage of extra fuel, the generation of a new flight plan, or some other strategy, it will be agreed upon, thus facilitating the departure.

STRATEGY and CONTINGENCIES.

The plan once agreed upon will be submitted with any amendments to many of the departments who initially provided information so they can monitor the flight's progress. If a change in the status of weather, airports or similar occurs enroute, the crew will be advised.

They will also proactively monitor the situation throughout the flight. The ability to construct a revised plan and "pivot" at short notice is essential in the dynamic environment of flight.

The crew will also assign each pilot a role, depending upon who is flying the sector, and each will already be aware of the associated responsibilities. Even so, a culture of cross-checking and support freely moves about the flight deck.

FINAL REVIEW.

Before the execution of any task with an element of finality, the crew will conduct a final review. Before the refueller disconnects the hose, is the fuel still sufficient based on the latest weather? Before the door is closed and the aerobridge is retracted, have all the ground staff left the aircraft?

In any organisation, the planning process will be generated at a deeper level across a range of sources that gather data. Armed with this data, the operational team can agree upon the goal they are tasked to achieve. They can then consider threats and mitigate against the risks, amending their strategy as needed to accommodate these contingencies. Before implementation, a final review can be undertaken to assess any interim changes.

Plan structures will differ; however, successful planning will come from the accuracy of the information provided and an environment that encourages input and questioning, regardless of rank. No-one plans to fail - they just fail to *plan properly*.

PROCESS

✈

Just Culture

Our times are plagued with catchphrases. Occasionally they endure, more frequently they fade with time, and in too many cases they simply confuse. One term, however, seems to have struck a chord with many - the concept of "culture".

Traditionally, the term culture was used to describe the ideas, customs and social behaviours for various societies around the world. In modern times the term was applied to those qualities as they exist within smaller entities, such as companies and organisations. Aviation took up the terminology and particularly used it concerning safety, or an airline's 'safety culture'. Still, an airline's culture can be even farther reaching, surfacing in aspects as varied as employee morale and customer relations.

The creation of an organisation's culture is challenging, particularly if a toxic culture needs to be dispensed within the first instance. To achieve this, the change must be led from the highest level of management and be led by example. It must reflect real behavioural change as opposed to a tick in the box and the announcement of a new arrival. For this to occur, such change must be a visible priority from senior management through to the most junior ranks. The management must genuinely endorse and encourage change and actively maintain it, rather than merely disseminating periodic memos and vague verbal assurances. And it begins with defining what an organisation wants to emphasise in its culture.

In aviation, safety is always paramount. For airlines, this means that management takes the time to sit down at safety meetings rather than being a perpetual 'apology' and asking for the Minutes to be left on their desk. In a thriving safety culture, self-reporting is considered as a professional act, rather than a confession of sins that may lead to purgatory. Again, this begins with management encouraging a "just culture", and this is a concept available to any company.

A "just culture" is one in which a mistake is seen as an opportunity to learn and not to punish. By not taking a punitive approach, personnel are more inclined to honestly report the real facts that led to the problem and not seek to disguise or deflect. It is only through understanding the real root cause of any issue that effective change can be made to avoid a repeat of the problem at a later date.

There will be an infrequent occasion where rogue behaviour or intentional non-compliance will occur, and that must be treated as a threat to the organisation, not an honest mistake. However, it usually will be an oversight by a team member doing their utmost but unfortunately not achieving the goal.

In a mature organisation, self-reporting is encouraged. Without fear of retribution, employees can put their hand up and take ownership of their shortcomings, and this can prove beneficial. In the immediate instance, the individual, team or crew can receive additional training and counselling. In a broader sense, reporting may reveal that this is not an isolated incident and can highlight a systemic problem within the organisation.

For self-reporting to occur, the organisation needs to establish a simple, accessible reporting system, with management taking an interest and ownership. Secondly, the organisation must encourage staff to be vigilant and report any threats that they may observe or any mishaps that have occurred. Equally, management must acknowledge and provide feedback to any report. Without feedback, the system will soon appear to be pointless, and participation will dwindle.

A just culture provides additional benefits to those stemming from a reporting system. It encourages communication of all types, both up and down the chain of command. Egos need to be checked at every level, allowing humility to facilitate open and honest discussion. In this way, employees won't take management's recommendations as a personal offence. Similarly, they will feel confident to communicate their observations from the operational level back up the chain to management. Through this technique, the free exchange of ideas can flow in both directions, and through this, the ownership of a concept is universal. The solution will be the result of consultation and consideration from a far broader range of perspectives.

A company's culture needs to permeate every aspect of its being. It must be evident in its image, and in its communications, both internal and with others. It must encourage the desired culture in the behaviour and operation of its people and the conduct of its processes.

Authentic, professional, skilled, just and "socially aware" are only a few qualities that a company may seek to integrate within their culture. Consider for a moment, the brands that spring to mind as reputable organisations and ask why. Is it an airline known for its safety record? For the skill level of its crews? For its proud heritage? Does it contribute to the broader community? Every organisation will be different n its goals, although there will undoubtedly be certain qualities that are foundation blocks.

From those foundation blocks, a company can only grow by embedding those qualities deeply into its culture, which will manifest through its people and operation. Companies with a sound and respected just culture have it instilled at all levels to the degree that it is not a conscious act but as natural as drawing breath. And when the employees and managers of such a company are asked why they operate in such a manner, the answer will be, "That's just what we do around here."

When every level of the company responds in this way, you know that the culture has found a home. The task moving forward is now to nurture and maintain.

PROCESS

Decision Making

Depending on the source, research indicates that an individual makes in the vicinity of 35,000 decisions each day. They can be as varied as which socks to wear, right through to which house to buy. Making decisions is a quality frequently associated with pilots, possibly as the operation of sophisticated machinery in the upper atmosphere suggests a complex environment. And it is. However, the decision-making process starts well before the wheels ever leave the ground and pilots are specifically trained in the "art" of decision-making.

As in everyday life, the issues demanding decisions from pilots may be straightforward, or they may be complicated. However, as with most aspects of airline operations, pilots are trained in a framework which can be applied to a range of scenarios. As we have seen throughout this book, the provision of a core framework offers a starting point to ward off procrastination and cues to draw in relevant information to, in turn, provide a timely outcome. Decision making is no different.

Air crews around the world use various models, but the most popular is attributed to Tony Kern, a United States Air Force veteran and specialist in the field of airmanship. His model, of which there are variants, is simple and known as **G.R.A.D.E**.

G – Gather information from every available source.

R – Review the Information, discarding what is not relevant and prioritising what remains.

A– Analyse the information and mitigate against risk.

D – Decide and initiate a course of action.

E – Evaluate the course of action. Is it working? If not, action an alternate plan.

Now let's consider the elements more closely.

G. Gather Information. It is important to gather all of the information available through the full range of resources. Compile data, ask questions and seek input from beyond the immediate circle of colleagues and crew.

R. Review the Information. Discard irrelevant data and opinions and organise the information into relevant topics. Prioritise the information within those topics and, in turn, prioritise those topics.

A. Analyse the Information. Consider the possible outcomes, both good and bad, and mitigate against unfavourable outcomes and risk. If the situation permits, test the information.

D. Decide on a Course of Action. Using the information and the projected possible outcomes, decide upon the course of action to be implemented.

E. Evaluate the Course of Action. Once implemented, review and confirm that the course of action is moving towards the goal. If not, does another plan need to be initiated, or the selected plan modified?

The implementation of GRADE will vary upon circumstances, just as it does for pilots. A fire breaking out after take-off will have straightforward considerations to be initiated in a minimal time frame. By comparison, should a passenger fall ill enroute, there may be time at hand to take notes and weigh up options. Can the crew seek medical support to diagnose the nature of the illness further? Is the condition time critical and is a diversion to a new destination required? The proximal airports may then be considered and culled based on runway length and whether local facilities have stairs that reach the aircraft door? What are the local health facilities?

The timeframe is a variable in all decision making that needs to be recognised. If time isn't a constraint, then don't be forced to rush – take a measured approach that is appropriate to the deadline. To do this, another element of decision-making must be called upon – to temper the emotions.

When challenged, it is easy to allow the adrenalin to kick in and to react irrationally, rather than proceed rationally. This human physiological response is discussed in "The Power of the Pause" and needs to be tempered. The first step is to stop for the moment and breathe. Oxygenate your brain and allow your brain to catch up with your body - which is being encouraged to fight or flee by its primal instincts.

Should we start to make our decisions before we have our bodily reactions under control, we are prone to hurry down an ill-considered path, rather than implement a process such as GRADE.

Furthermore, it is yet another time when an organisation's culture and training can emerge from its passive position to take on an active role. Firstly, it does this by allowing people to speak openly and question, with tact. Possibly using the "Managing Upwards" technique of C.A.I.R, that is covered elsewhere in this book. Secondly, if alone, training teaches us to pause, step back to the "jumpseat" and take in the bigger picture, allowing us to be self-critical in a constructive way.

Decision making is a part of our everyday life in which most minor choices are resolved with minimal thought and consideration. However, when those choices and their ramifications become more substantial, a systematic framework, such as GRADE, is a tool that can be employed. For the best outcome, it must be a tool that is used in a timely, measured fashion and not thrown out in anger or panic. A cool head and a calm process will yield the best results.

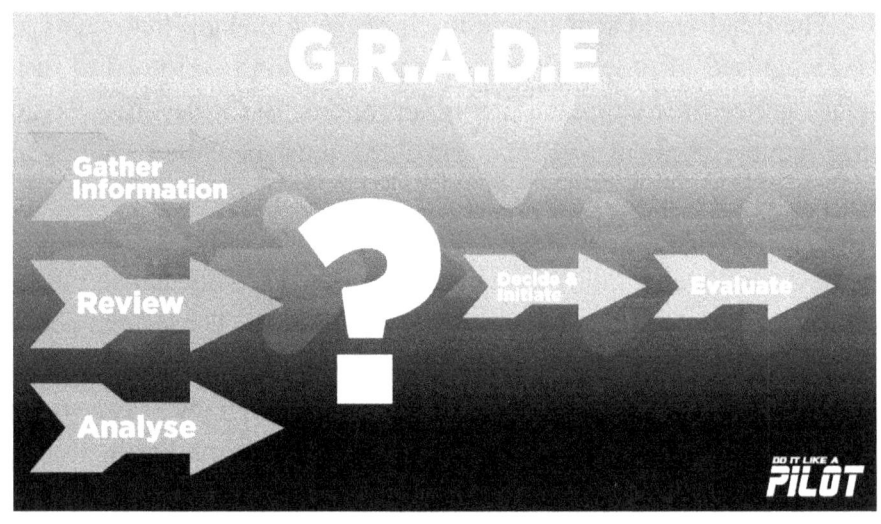

PROCESS

✈

Check And Training

There are many aspects of airline operations that contribute to its enviable safety record, but undoubtedly one of the key points is the environment of ongoing "Check and Training". A career in the field requires an ongoing commitment to learning. While the adage may reflect that "you never know it all", the reality is that very little is left to chance when it comes to a pilot's level of knowledge.

As a student pilot, a good deal of theory comes before the practical application of a skill. And then, competency must be demonstrated before the fledgling pilot is trusted to undertake that skill alone in the air. Even when deemed competent, that skill will be verified, or "checked" at regular intervals and should an absence from flying occur for any period; they will be called to demonstrate their competency all over again. This is the same for the most senior of airline captains.

Depending upon the airline, in qualifying to fly another type of aircraft an experienced airline pilot will typically undertake six weeks of ground school. A similar time is then spent flying exercises in a flight simulator and then a month, or more, flying the aircraft with a training captain. When deemed to be of a satisfactory standard, they then must be "checked to the line", by an appropriately named, "Check Captain". At every stage, they will be asked to recall memory items, quizzed on policies and procedures, aircraft systems, rules and regulations.

As a qualified line pilot, they will be called to display their competency in the simulator four times each year and an annual "route check" in the aircraft. There will also be many days of ground school training encompassing everything from "Human Factors" in aircraft accidents and the use of emergency equipment to understanding the company's "Drug and Alcohol Policy". It would be unusual to have a period of greater than six weeks, where some aspect of the pilot's knowledge is not formally challenged.

It sounds rigorous, and it can be. And with one's livelihood on the line, passing each time is far from assured although further training is the usual response to a failed exercise rather than an axe being wielded.

In recent times, "Checking" has even taken on a different outlook to thirty years ago when the environment almost seemed punitive at best on occasions. The expression "Checking with a 'T' for Training" is often used in the modern training environment and recognises that while standards need to be maintained, a "check" is also an opportunity for learning and growth. A further byproduct of the ongoing training is that it provides an opportunity to reinforce the latest changes in the operation, even if they have been promulgated in company documentation. Additionally, and importantly, it is another means by which operational crews can provide feedback to the company.

Within an airline, that training extends far beyond pilots. Every department has some form of training regime, and often there are sections where the practice overlaps. Pilots will sometimes undergo training alongside flight attendants, offering each a greater insight into the other's role while enhancing communication and teamwork in normal operations and emergencies. As well as cross-department training, bringing in external personnel safeguards against becoming too insular and operating in "a bubble".

These days, regular visits to the flight simulator for training are increasingly "evidence-based". That is to say that airlines are now observing trends across the airline in terms of reported incidents and drilling down on potential weaknesses, rather than just addressing a routine checklist of items. The training also factors in past performances of the individual pilot, ensuring that maximum benefit is forthcoming. Even when fully qualified on a new aircraft type, the prudent pilot will attentively and humbly listen to junior pilots who have more experience on that type.

The issue of relevant training continues into relevant experience. There is no blank acceptance that skills from one aircraft type, or one airline, to another is necessarily transferable. To the contrary, even the most experienced pilot will readily check their ego and accept the role of the student. Similarly, if an employee has served with an organisation in a role for an extended period, that experience may not bear relevance should they move elsewhere.

Even in an age when airliners are heavily automated and possess an enviable safety record, the core piloting skills are reinforced in simulator training through artificially degrading systems. As with many industries, the increasing reliance on automation leaves pilots vulnerable should a need to manually fly their aircraft be required. The safeguard is training for such an eventuality and have procedures in place; whether on the flight deck or the factory floor.

In many organisations, the training structure may not be so formal and "checking" may not even exist. There may be a requirement to test a building's evacuation procedures in the case of fire, but general preparedness for the unexpected does not necessarily extend much further. Training is sometimes better catered for although it can remain solely in the realm of the motivated individual who pursues courses outside of business hours.

A commonly quoted hurdle for inhouse training is cost and downtime for employees, but as the saying in aviation circles goes, *"If you think safety is expensive, try having an accident."*

As discussed in the chapter titled "Pre-Mortem", pilots make it their regular practice to envisage the worst-case scenario and prepare a strategy in advance. In the flight simulator, these strategies aren't merely considered; they are tested in incredibly realistic circumstances. All of the associated warning lights and bells, sounds and motions are replicated in association with realistic displays projected up the simulator's "windscreen". The realism not only creates the situation but evokes mental and physical responses from the pilots - and just like the execution of procedures, these too can be trained.

Bringing some level of training and checking in-house within an organisation can provide genuine benefits. Just as a "boot camp" can bring people together so too can a training day. Once there, open discussion can be taken from the water cooler to a more formal environment, facilitating valuable feedback, converting anonymous complaints into constructive criticism. Furthermore, it is an opportunity to introduce a standardised approach to the operation and reinforce the company culture. As discussed in the chapters on SOPs and creating culture, this is far more than a catch-cry. It is about having a common expectation and a shared mental model, thus highlighting any divergence from this path. This is a means of making communication more efficient and critically, offers a technique to identify possible problems at an early stage before they can escalate.

Training is more than merely imposing theoretical knowledge for the sake of it. A greater understanding allows all employees to take a greater stake in the process and provide them with the tools to identify faults better and troubleshoot problems. A pilot does not necessarily need to know how the aircraft's air conditioning system works but when the smell of smoke leaks into the cabin but not the cockpit, an informed pilot can potentially identify the source and set about addressing the issue in conjunction with their training and a checklist.

In addition to training, checking a company's processes and standards at regular intervals can also provide a benefit and an opportunity for improvement. It can also capture a decaying situation and rectify it before it suffers a damaging consequence. It must be noted that in this day of audits and Key Performance Indicators (KPIs), we must remember, that sometimes things of value cannot be measured, while at other times the process is caught up measuring things of little value.

Unfortunately, shortcomings in training and standards may only become evident when things go wrong, and this is never truer than in aviation. However, this is also true for companies, and they can also benefit from ongoing training and periodically checking standards. Bedding in company culture, good communication across the organisation and improving standards will not "just happen", and training is the key. As they say, *"If you think safety is expensive, try having an accident."*

PROCESS

Warning Signs

"WHOEVER SEES IT - CALLS IT."

Modern airliners are designed to advise the flight crew of problems with their systems as they arise. As not all issues constitute an emergency, so there are varying levels of notification generated – they may even be colour-coded. This tiered information allows a pilot to address the problem appropriately and prioritise the required tasks, for in a critical situation more than one fault may be in play. Depending on the aircraft, the indications are divided into three categories – an advisory, a caution or a warning.

In the first case, the notification draws the crew's attention to the system that requires attention. Furthermore, the type of indication conveys the level of intervention and the level of urgency.

An *advisory* may simply notify the pilots that a minor system fault exists, such as it momentarily operating outside of its normal parameters, or its fluid level requires "topping up". No immediate action is needed to be taken, although on occasions an advisory can be a precursor to a greater problem. If displayed as a colour-coded message, an advisory is generally in white text.

A *caution* will notify the pilots that there is an issue requiring their intervention. It calls for an operating procedure or technique, and the failure to do so may result in damage to equipment. If displayed as a colour-coded message, or a light, a caution is generally amber and accompanied by an audible chime.

A *warning* will also notify the pilots that there is an issue requiring their intervention. However, it calls for an operating procedure or technique, and the failure to do so may result in personal injury or the loss of life. If displayed as a colour-coded message, or a light, a warning is generally red and accompanied by a loud horn or bells.

As always, when an event beyond the norm occurs, there is the chance of being startled and our initial response is in danger of being overly rapid and reactive. Pause and take a breath to let the brain's logic pathways to resume command. This moment is also an opportunity to check the ego and consider, "What did I just do?"

With each increasing level of severity, the notification becomes more apparent and calls for a more significant course of action. Crews respond immediately and as a team, with their roles pre-defined. An advisory, caution or warning will be cross-checked and confirmed by both pilots before any notification is cleared, extinguished or silenced.

Outside of the flight deck, life and business do not possess warning horns and colour-coded messages to advise us when systems are breaking down, although our approach can benefit by replicating that of the flight deck. Keep the aircraft flying safely and then – Identify, Verify, Rectify.

In doing so, prioritisation is important. A crew will not overly focus on an advisory that recommends that a tyre is becoming low on pressure, while bells and lights are flashing to indicate an engine fire. They will prioritise. In a business, attending to an email that requires a reply by the following week should not take precedence over a critical deadline.

There are many issues, even in normal operations, that pilots are called to prioritise, and it is a skill set that is always exercised. Additionally, some procedures are not annunciated and not cued by any system of messages, lights or sounds. Frequently because the symptoms are obvious, such as a landing gear lever that is jammed, or smoke in the cockpit. With multiple issues, the crew will consider the problem linked most directly to the potentially worst outcome and prioritise from there. Any fire or a flight control issue is always critical.

When an advisory, caution or warning occurs, it is not necessarily the captain that sees it and the expression of, "Whoever sees it – calls it" is commonplace on the flight deck. In the same way, a manager cannot be expected to be across every aspect of an organisation at ground level at all times. The company culture should encourage open two-way communication where any employee at any level can recognise and advise of a problem they foresee or detect. And such an initiative should be encouraged and then recognised when it occurs.

Importantly, the categories of advisory, caution and warning have been pre-defined. They have been assessed in the calm of a planning room at the aircraft manufacturer's plant, not in the rarified upper atmosphere by a crew under pressure. Similarly, a manager can prioritise tasks when they first come across the desk before the deadline is looming. Some even categorise them in order of timeframe, or the level of employee or manager needed. Like the flight deck, the tasks can even be assigned a colour. A "Red" task requires immediate action, an "Amber" task within the week and a "Blue" task within the month – or whichever system suits the organisation.

The colour-coding can become embedded in the language of the company and even its documentation. Like standard operating procedures, when they are promulgated and actioned from the top down, they are more easily adopted.

It is important to note that issues can "jump" categories if the situation worsens. An undetectable engine vibration on an aircraft may manifest as an advisory, only to escalate to an engine fire when a wayward component comes loose. In a company, deadlines can shift in both directions. A "blue" task may move up the chain to become "red", just as an urgent task can be postponed. Once again, when the language is universal, the understanding is clear across the organisation.

Systems that can warn of impending or immediate issues are another means of creating a level of efficiency. They provide the first level of diagnosis and call for the appropriate level of intervention, whether that is on a flight deck or in an office. Not all issues will come with an associated warning, and the identification will fall upon the individual or crew. And not all problems will be seen first by the captain, so "Whoever sees it – calls it."

A system indicating a degree of urgency and the required action in the first instance is a worthwhile practice. It will still call for the issue to be positively identified and verified before that action takes place, but it sets the wheels in motion and begins the process of prioritising. In this way, the operation continues to move forward.

PROCESS

Rejected Take-Offs And Unstable Approaches

It is not a perfect world, and not every take-off and landing are without event. The cause may have been beyond our control, or it may be the result of our actions. Either way, regret is not a strategy and time can be a luxury that we do not have, particularly on the flight deck.

The take-off and approach to land are critical phases of flight. With the proximity of the ground and all that is happening, it is of no surprise these times are when many inflight incidents occur.

On take-off, we are endeavouring to accelerate a craft designed for air travel to a speed on the ground generally reserved for racing cars to generate enough airflow over the wings to create lift. At a time when the aircraft is heavy with the weight of its fuel load, it will most likely not have sufficient runway length to achieve flying speed and still come to a safe halt should something cause us to conduct a "Rejected Take-Off", or RTO.

However, a speed can be calculated to offer both options – either an RTO or a take-off. At this nominated speed, the crew can perform a series of actions that will bring the aircraft to a halt on the remaining runway. At or beyond that speed, even if one of the engines has failed, the aircraft can continue to accelerate, achieve flying speed, take-off and remain clear of the surrounding obstacles and terrain.

This speed is officially termed as "V1", colloquially referred to as a "Go, No-Go Speed" and importantly considered to be a "Decision Speed".

Well before taking off, the V1 is calculated by considering a range of variables that include the aircraft weight, the runway surface, wind conditions, temperature, air pressure and the terrain, as well as any issues with the aircraft that may degrade its performance. As with all aspects of airline operations, a "buffer" is applied to the calculation, and ultimately a V1 speed is determined. This process was once calculated by referring to a large book of runway charts and pilots would run their pencil along the "X" and "Y" axis, cross-referring to a wavy line and eventually ascertain a speed. Today, an even more accurate calculation is achieved instantly through Apps on electronic devices. For safety, the speed is calculated independently by each pilot on the flight deck, before they cross-check and verify their results.

Armed with a V1 speed, the crew will brief which technical and environmental problems will call for a rejected take-off, as in the case of a minor event it is safer to continue the take-off. They will then review their actions for an issue occurring before V1 and at, or beyond, V1. These actions have been trained many times in the simulator and recalling them is done by memory, not by checklist, as they must be recalled and implemented without hesitation.

A V1, or decision speed, is a concept that can be applied to a range of undertakings outside of aviation. Importantly, this point of decision is calculated unemotionally and well in advance of the event taking place. It has considered the current environment and future obstacles should the plan continue, albeit with degraded performance. Sometimes, the situation will be limited by the environment or terrain, so weight may need to be shed to achieve flight safely.

When we are planning a personal or business decision, calculating at which future point we should reject the plan, or continue, is a prudent strategy. Furthermore, doing so by drawing in every relevant piece of information at a time when we are not time-compressed or under pressure, offers a far more balanced and unemotional decision.

Carrying the concept through, we can consider what obstacles may be in our way should we continue the plan. Are we going to be required to carry on with reduced financial or human resources? Will they be sufficient to sustain us on the path ahead? Once again, the "pre-mortem" concept of considering the worst-case scenario allows us to be prepared, rather than relying on hope.

The approach to land is another situation where defining parameters in advance permits a sound, safe decision, void of emotion. As with a take-off, an approach to land can be interrupted by unforeseen technical or environmental issues. Erratic winds known as "Windshear", or a wind across the runway with a strength beyond the limits of the aircraft, or a heavy shower of rain reducing visibility can call for the landing to be abandoned. When flying the aircraft solely with reference to instruments on approach, many runways will require that the pilots break out of cloud and see the runway with adequate time to conduct a landing. Again, if this does not occur, it is time to abandon the approach to land.

The pilots can find their aircraft in an awkward position in the three dimensions, quite possibly through their flight management. They may be too high, calling for the final descent to the runway to be too steep to be safe. They may be flying too fast, requiring more runway to land than they have calculated or have available. They may be too low and lack enough clearance from the terrain. They may not be aligned with the runway early enough, making it difficult to achieve a wings level landing. They may be unable to achieve "touchdown" in the safe landing zone. There may be other undesirable states of flight as well that challenge the opportunity to land the aircraft safely. In these situations, the approach is called "unstable", and just as if the weather had intervened, the landing must be rejected. A manoeuvre called a "Go-Around" or "Missed Approach" is then flown. The aircraft is climbed away to a safe height for the crew to brief once again and reposition for another approach.

It is worth noting that even after touchdown, a landing can be abandoned, the aircraft can fly away, and another attempt made. On most aircraft, only when the engines are selected to "reverse thrust" to assist the aircraft stopping is the aircraft truly committed to landing. In the process of executing a plan in an organisation, the same can apply. Working out the latest point at which an initial plan should be abandoned and reconsidered is best calculated calmly and in advance.

In this broad range of situations, there are pre-defined quantitative parameters, that should an aircraft venture outside them, a go-around is required. As with the rejected take-off, these parameters are calculated and considered well in advance. They are published limits. Minimum levels of visibility, minimum cloud base and maximum crosswinds. Maximum rates of descent, maximum tolerances on planned airspeed, limits on the touchdown zone. All calculated well before and all non-negotiable.

Both pilots must monitor these limits, and if they are not achieved, then a go-around is called for. The support pilot is required to speak up and call the limit, and the pilot flying is required to respond. And if the call of "unstable" is made the pilot flying must go-around. The call and response must be without hesitation, regardless of the rank and experience levels involved. Junior pilots are required to tell the senior captain to go-around, and in turn, they must respond.

Just as these limits are pre-defined, airline culture can play a role in advance. Ego can be an obstacle to a go-around, making a pilot hesitant to admit that they have not flown the approach correctly, with a go-around perceived as a failure. This is not the case - a go-around is recognition of an unsafe state, and a professional will check the ego and place their passengers and task first. As discussed in "Culture", an airline creates an environment that encourages an approach to be abandoned if any doubt exists. A "Just Culture" states that punitive action will not be taken in the event of a go-around. It will need to be reported for learning, and it may call for further crew training, but a professional airline environment will not seek to punish a less than ideal approach if it is aborted.

Sound decision-making is aided by forethought and planning. By unemotionally calculating the limiting parameters of any task in advance dispels ambiguity and the temptation to "push on" when pressure and overwhelm raise their heads. Those limits may have a rapid onset, or slowly and insidiously evolve. Either way, the limits remain constant and a trigger for the plan to be modified with a go-around - and a second approach, as previously agreed. Just as the advantage of time and planning has benefits, a company's culture is pivotal in encouraging the decisions to be made without ego or fear of retribution. When an unfavourable situation is abandoned early enough, the opportunity to try again will remain.

PROCESS

✈ Finding The Gaps

Perfection is the stuff of throwaway lines and fairy tales, while the pursuit of excellence is ongoing. Airline operations around the world is a clear example of this and is reinforced by the statistics that show it to be the safest form of travel. Critical in the search for "the good" is discovery of "the bad" – or at least what could be done better. It is in this domain that aviation has a long-established strategy.

Known as briefing, a crew will discuss the salient points of a phase of flight. It may be prior to departure or before an approach to land is made. Its goal is to be "brief" and particularly highlight any variations to the norm. Many companies discuss potential change in meetings before implementing a course of action, however, airline crews excel at immediately reviewing what has happened, known as "debriefing".

When established in cruise flight, pilots will discuss how the departure could have been better handled, what was handled well, any omissions, or unusual events that occurred. They will repeat the process after parking the aircraft, normally with the captain challenging the crew to raise points and then discussing how these can be mitigated against in future. If it involves a significant or newly discovered issue, a formal report will be submitted to the company for the flight operations department to consider.

The" debrief" needs to be succinct and immediate to capture the relevant points while they are fresh in the mind. Once listed, they can be addressed again and, in more detail, later if needed. However, the first key is to identify the **"GAPS"**.

G – Gather the information.

A – Assess the facts.

P – Perform a "Post-mortem"

S – Identify the shortfall between the outcome and the original goal.

G. Gather the Information. As it is a "briefing" – keep it brief. Encourage input from the most junior participants, possibly by asking them to contribute first. There will generally be a few points that could be improved upon. Silence may be an indication that no-one wishes to criticise the captain or manager. In this instance, the manager needs to take the lead and suggest something that they, themselves could have done better. However, if there is still silence, it may indicate that nothing needs to be said, so recognise the fact and move on. In a positive sense, it may be an opportunity to recognise why the process went smoothly as it is equally important to recognise and then replicate success.

A. Assess the Facts. Discuss the facts that have been raised. Some misconceptions and misunderstandings can be explained at this point to refine the information down into the actual events that need to be addressed.

P. Perform a Post-mortem. With the now-shortened list, discuss why the events may have occurred. What was the actual effect? What was potentially the worst outcome?

S. Identify the Shortfall. Identify the shortfall, or "GAPS", between the actual outcome and the planned goal. Negative and positive variations should be reported to highlight shortcomings and reinforce successes.

How can the process be improved in the future or the shortfall mitigated against? Has the shortfall been witnessed before by anyone in attendance? – this may be an indication of a systemic, organisational issue. Would reporting the shortfall, and even suggesting a remedy, be worthwhile? Was there a positive lesson learned?

Completion of a project is not a time to rest on laurels, it is a time to review and report while the details are still readily at hand. Finding the GAPS is a healthy process that benefits directly from a culture of open and just communication, regardless of rank and standing. It is also a worthwhile personal process and many pilots at the end of the day will review their day and target three things that they could have done better. It is important not to be too harsh on oneself, or the process can be counterproductive. The individual can start to doubt their own competency and erode their confidence, and this is not the goal. It is merely a positive recognition of the reality that we can all always do better.

GAPS is equally relevant in a briefing before initiating a plan, although in place of a post-mortem, we substitute a pre-mortem. As discussed, in another chapter, this is where we conceive the worst possible outcome and mitigate against it in advance. In Part Two, we will revisit the GAPS concept and the integral role that it plays in the ongoing cycle of management.

Except in the exceedingly rare instance of rogue behaviour and intentional malicious intent, mistakes and shortfalls in our plans are due to honest mistakes and oversights. Ignoring their existence leaves the issue unaddressed with the potential to escalate. Finding the GAPS is about identifying and resolving issues, good and bad, for the future as we continue our unending pursuit of excellence.

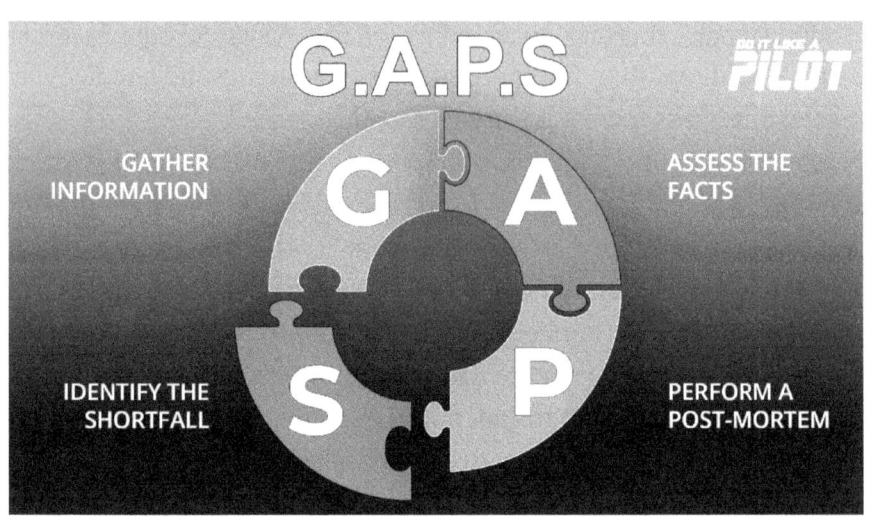

PROCESS

✈

CREATING A DIVERSION

There are occasions when the best-laid plans can't achieve their intended goal at first. For pilots, circumstances may intervene that preclude an arrival at the planned destination and an in-flight diversion to another airport is required. Just as the environment an airliner passes through can change, so can the market in which a company operates. The ability to be adaptable and pivot with minimal advance notice is not just a desirable trait in this modern world – it is essential.

The perception is that airline operations are rigidly structured. It is a world of procedures, checklists, schedules and uniforms. While this is true, it is this organised structure that affords it the ability to change its plans, possibly with minimal time available and occasionally under the duress of an emergency. It is adaptability born of structure.

This book has discussed the pre-mortem process in detail and the strategy of planning for contingencies. In doing so, the pilots have confirmed that adequate resources are available - such as fuel and a runway upon which to land. The consideration in advance of the "What ifs?" provides a pre-made plan, which in turn removes a degree of uncertainty – things can still change.

Strategies planned in advance can cover a range of eventualities, including engine failure and a loss of cabin pressurisation. Even how far from a particular airport an aircraft can fly before it no longer has the fuel to return and another airport must be considered. This is known as the Point of No Return, or PNR.

However, no amount of forward planning can cater for every situation. The unexpected closure of a runway when the aircraft landing ahead becomes disabled, or an unforecast fog rolls in, making an entire airport unavailable. The possibilities are too many to draft a checklist or procedure for every scenario and access to communications with ground-based support may be available, but it may not. The pilots are trained and expected to adapt and overcome independently in what is effectively a working example of "decentralised command".

The crew understands that safety must be their first consideration, but beyond that, the airline entrusts them to seek out a means to achieve the goal independently. They are also aware of the commercial ramifications of a diversion when gathering information to make their decision. Although rather than commercial considerations being the driving force behind a decision, they are more likely to play a role when assessing the options available.

Depending on the nature of the event, that may mean a diversion to land briefly for what is termed a "tech stop" to load additional fuel and continue. In this case, the planned destination may still be achievable. A critically ill passenger may necessitate rerouting to the nearest medical facilities. A significant systems failure may require that the aircraft land as soon as possible, anywhere that the runway is long enough.

In an emergency, the crew will be under even greater duress. Their time in the air is limited by how much fuel is in the tanks. The flying characteristics of the aircraft may be compromised and even worsen when wheels and flaps are lowered for landing. Or the warnings on the flight deck indicate a problem, but the severity is unknown. The plan needs to change - and it may need to change quickly.

If it is an event that has contingency planning in place, then the process will be relatively straightforward. Other situations will draw in more variables. Regardless, it will be a structured approach that facilitates flexibility.

Aviate – Navigate – Communicate. Keep the aircraft in a safe state of flight.

Procedures and checklists will be used to address any systems problem. The time available will be calculated. Airports within that timeframe, or fuel range, will be shortlisted, their weather conditions, availability and any other possible limitations checked. Any further information that can be gathered will be drawn from any available source. This step forms the "G" in the GRADE decision-making process. A process that will be used to decide the course of action. The planning of the diversion is part of a structured process, even though the inputs and the outcomes are varied. The process does not only offer efficiency but by utilising a "known" when investigating the "unknowns", releases mental capacity. There is order, a shared mental model and mutual expectations between the crew as well as defined duties. These have all been trained in well before the fateful flight.

Firstly, the organisation must be kept flying safely and not become distracted or fixated on the task. "Decentralised command", training and processes can be equally effective at ground level when a change in direction is called for with minimal notice. There must be faith from management in the crew at the coal face to make choices in accordance with their training and the company's culture, objectives and priorities. Once headed in the new direction, a review of the situation offers the opportunity to refine or modify the plan.

It should also be considered that despite forward planning and consideration, unforeseen diversions can be forced upon an organisation with minimal warning, too. Again, we look to Sullenberger's forced landing on the Hudson River. Deprived of engine power, his time was finite. In such a situation, a pilot goes "Big to Small". Keep the aircraft flying, identify the most obvious, satisfactory option and execute the plan. Do not become fixated on an unnecessary task but always attend to the major issue.

There is also an expression among pilots to, "Fly the aircraft into the accident." It is not an act of pessimism – in fact, it is the opposite. It means to never accept that everything that can be done, has been done and relinquish control to fate. Even if an aircraft were to start ploughing through a field, maintain control, there still may be trees to be avoided. In a broader, less dramatic sense, it means to continue to work the problem and *never* give up.

The original plan will always set out the most desired objective and the ideal strategy to achieve it. However, when the environment changes, often those that can adapt most quickly achieve the best outcomes and with the greatest reserves of resources. The flexibility to do so can come from a solid base. Flight crew structures that are designed to offer efficiency, calm and considered planning at 38,000 feet are readily adapted whenever there is a need to divert from the original plan.

PEOPLE

Much More Than Pilots

Since the tragic events of 9/11, pilots are generally hidden behind a bulletproof flight deck door. The days of allowing visitors to the cockpit, or even to remain for the landing are long gone. And it's a shame for both parties. Today, the best that passengers can hope for is a glimpse of the pilots walking through the gate lounge or seated in an airport terminal coffee shop, but the interaction is minimal. Even so, pilots tend to remain the face of an airline.

The reality is that the pilots are just one element of a far greater and complex organism. To watch a time-lapse video on YouTube of an airliner arriving at the terminal, being serviced and then departing offers some insight into that complexity and the broader scope of people that are involved. Refuellers, baggage handlers, cleaners, engineers, flight attendants and airport managers are all moving about in an orchestrated series of moves to prepare the aircraft for another flight.

While these departments may all have different roles, their interdependence is critical. The flight attendants cannot board the passengers until the cabin is cleaned and they have additional requirements if refuelling is in progress. The engineer may be called upon to supervise that refuelling process, which cannot begin until the pilots have relayed how much fuel they require. That information is needed by those calculating the overall weight of the aircraft and organising the loading so that the aircraft stays "in balance". Not too much weight to the rear, making it tail heavy, and similarly not too much down the front. And balance must be maintained throughout the flight as fuel is used.

Should any one department operate without communicating with the others, the process will be delayed at best and miss a critical point of safety at worst. This was demonstrated in a failed incentive scheme at one airline.

Airline management devised a small financial incentive for each departure that left on time. It was just a few dollars to each ground staff member involved with that particular flight, although over a month, those dollars could add up. What eventuated was chaos driven by understandable self-interest.

All that the baggage handlers wanted to do was close the doors to the cargo hold. The engineers pestered the pilots incessantly for the fuel order and gritted their teeth if there was an issue with the aircraft that needed attention. Those organizing the loading and balance of the aircraft just wanted to sign off on their data and send it through, and often this was done prematurely. And the manager dispatching the flight wishing to shut the door as quickly as possible, regardless of what was happening in the cabin. It was a mess.

The door was shut while flight attendants were still trying to stow carry-on luggage, frequently calling for the aerobridge to be reconnected and the door opened for over-sized baggage to be stored in the hold. Cargo holds were closed with bags left behind unnecessarily, and incorrect loading paperwork had to be resubmitted and recalculated. There were numerous communication breakdowns as everyone lost their appreciation of being part of a team. In simple terms, "haste was waste", and it grew from a plan to make the process more efficient.

By comparison, in normal operations, the various players combine with an awareness of where they fit in compared to the other elements. They understand how one issue can have a cascading effect if it is not communicated and addressed. People don't need to be able to undertake the other tasks but is an advantage to have a basic understanding, and nowhere is this more evident than on the flight deck.

It is here that the captain and crew draw the information and required actions together and act as a conduit to raise concerns and relay information. The pilots don't have to hold the end of the fuel hose, load bags into the cargo hold or clean the cabin. To do so would tie them unnecessarily to a single task and draw their leadership away from a broader focus. But they do need to understand what is involved. This offers an appreciation of the time required, thereby assisting in the smooth execution of the process. It also provides an insight that is invaluable in troubleshooting when things go awry. No-one expects anyone to know everything about everything – even the captain - but in a senior management role, you should have a core understanding.

Additionally, as a leader, appreciating the role of each contributing department can dispel the aloofness that can be perceived regarding leadership positions. Just as a manager can walk the factory floor or the administration department's hallways, a captain pausing to discuss the role of a team member makes them feel valued, as they rightly should. Taking such opportunities to make genuine contact with members of a team has another positive effect in that it opens the way for honest two-way communication and timely feedback is vital to any manager. Only the success of each individual within the team can permit the overall success, and a leader's humility can go a long way to making this happen.

As the role becomes closer to a manager's core task, the subordinate's duties require even greater understanding. A captain needs to be clear on a flight attendant's duties and timings to manage such things as the seat belt sign and cabin service as it relates to turbulence that may lay ahead. More importantly, what their roles would be in an emergency. Closer still, the captain must understand the co-pilot's role and responsibilities intimately to ensure that crew coordination is at its best and no task is overlooked.

For any organisation to work at its peak efficiency, it needs to be appreciated that many people contribute to the success. Even if that success is routinely attributed to the leader, a leader must understand the roles of those in support. With that level of knowledge becoming greater as that position grows ever-closer to their own. This is made easier if the leader checks their ego and displays humility and respect towards their team.

A successful flight needs much more than pilots.

PEOPLE

✈

What Is Command?

For many, Captain Chesley Sullenberger personifies what it is to be an airline captain. Following the "Miracle on the Hudson" when he effectively glided the Airbus airliner to a safe water landing after striking a flock of geese, Sully became known around the world. Always humble, he was inclusive of the efforts of the crew despite the media continually focusing the spotlight solely on him. And while the execution was impeccable, there was more to the "miracle" than purely Sully's manipulative flying skills.

The entire flight lasted 208 seconds – from take-off to touchdown. In that time, he and his co-pilot had to fly the aircraft, attempt to trouble-shoot the problem and restart the engines. They had to communicate with air traffic control, and the passengers, all the while reviewing the options for a safe landing. And let's not forget, he and his crew were doing all of this calmly in the face incredible odds.

Even when the aircraft was safely stopped in the water, Sully remained a captain – concerned for the passengers and crew above all else. No wonder he was heralded as a hero. An accolade that he readily redirected to his entire crew. However, the airline captain has not always shared this profile.

The rise of commercial airlines after World War Two saw many former military pilots slip straight into the role of airline captain. With the change they brought the authoritarian mindset that a combat pilot needed. Often gaining their command of a bomber at a tender age, they were entrusted with the lives of their young crew in an extremely hostile environment. Decisions were made, orders followed, and questions were not asked. Many bombers carried only a single pilot and fighter pilots operated alone in their cockpits. The mission came before any concern for personal safety and, in an emergency, all eyes were turned to the captain. And from the captain all instructions flowed.

It was only in the 1970s and as a result of a series of accidents that the situation began to change – and it was generational change. Philosophies such as Crew Resource Management (CRM) began to evolve, recognising that the captain was a manager and was well advised to be inclusive of the crew. The final command responsibility still rested with the captain, but they were now encouraged to draw input from, and delegate duties to, their crew.

The cockpit is still potentially a management crucible with life-threatening decisions, but the role of command has changed on the modern flight deck. That day in New York when Sully's airliner was crippled, he flew the aircraft, but the team worked together to see their passengers survive. No old-style captain could have barked enough commands, made the decisions and flown the aircraft in a way to match the way that Sully and his crew worked co-operatively – over less than four minutes.

The principles of leadership and management that we use in our lives and our business have much in common with those of a modern airline captain. However, the cockpit is a dynamic environment with a finite timeframe that is limited to the fuel available for flight – or even less in an emergency. Yet in this crucible, that is moving at close to the speed of sound; we need to remain calm, communicate effectively, plan and execute competently to ensure a safe outcome for the lives entrusted to our care.

In our workplace, the stakes at risk may be different, but they can still be high. Regardless of the context, certain qualities define a leader, and these qualities can be executed successfully or poorly. In this first chapter, we will consider those qualities that are to be found in leaders and in subsequent chapters we will examine the good, the bad and the ugly of how those qualities are put into action.

Communicative.

Every course, coaching session and book on leadership and management stresses the importance of communication, and yet it remains an ongoing problem. Communication is multi-tiered and two-way. A captain needs to adapt their language to the situation, time frame and the audience. How a conversation will run with an 18-year-old cabin crew member is entirely different from responding to an air traffic controller's instruction. Accordingly, the captain must tailor their language to the audience and the situation. Furthermore, they need a response to confirm that the message has been received. In critical scenarios, they will often have the crew member read back the main points.

Communication is the connectivity in a leader's toolbox. The greatest concept or most fundamental instruction is severely compromised if it cannot be effectively conveyed. Even more critically, an incorrectly received message can do damage that can call for additional time and resources to recover. Sometimes, in business and in flight, recovery may not be possible.

Competent.

Some captains are great communicators, incredible with their crew and even fantastic in the planning phase. However, their basic flying skills and flight management are lacking. The airline training and checking system filters out these pilots and, sadly, they can lose their command status, demoted to the co-pilot role.

In any leadership role, a level of competency is required. Without this, the team will not have confidence in their leader no matter how satisfactorily they manage their people. Ultimately, a leader needs to use every resource at their disposal efficiently to get the job done but only so much can be delegated. A shortfall in ability can undermine the entire process, and that is why the selection and training of leaders is an essential step in the process.

Calm.

Panic and fear are contagious. Regardless of the emergency that is confronting them, a captain must maintain their composure to both retain command of the situation and maintain clarity of thought. When the chips are down, everyone will look to the captain, and they don't need to see someone having an emotional melt-down. That is not to say that a captain is not affected, but they need to maintain perspective and keep emotions in check.

There will inevitably be a 'startle effect' when the bells start ringing, and lights start flashing red in the cockpit. That surge of adrenalin and increased heart rate dates back to our primitive roots, and the 'fight or flight' reflex. Pilots are trained in this and encouraged to pause – or "sit on their hands" for a moment. This allows the instinct to subside and logical resolution to start regaining control of the brain.

In the day to day of life or business, there will be emergencies great and small. As a manager or a parent, we need to remain calm no matter how great the desire is to lash out. Emotive responses are not only frequently incorrectly tied to ongoing regret, but the impact upon those around the leader in a negative way. They can effectively close down communication channels until the calm has returned.

A leader needs to create an environment where honest and open feedback can be expressed, and one who flies into fits of rage scares off this feedback and potentially misses out on vital information at a vital time. The tension that fills the air can be infectious, leading to a less than ideal home or workplace.

The techniques, tactics and strategies adopted by captains and co-pilots alike are discussed throughout this book, but here are some universal qualities to consider.

Consultative.

Nobody knows everything about everything and a captain must have the humility to recognise this. For all the years of study and experience, a captain still cannot know every single element of engineering that relates to the aircraft or every task that every cabin crew member needs to perform.

Metaphorically, the cockpit door needs to be open so that the captain can seek out information and, in turn, others can seek information from the captain. It is this pooling of the knowledge base and open exchange of ideas that aid decision-making and leads to the best outcomes. Air crew are trained in the skill under the title of 'Crew Resource Management' or CRM – a topic we will examine in detail later in the book.

Importantly, it is the captain who establishes the environment and sets the tone for CRM to take place.

Caring.

A captain is responsible for the welfare of the passengers and crew alike. In turn, cabin crew can include excited teenagers fresh out of school, or single mums, desperate to get home to their kids. Finances may be a concern, and the cancellation of a flight may impact their pay packet. Being aware of fatigue levels and the crew's safety for their drive home. The range of considerations can be vast.

While a captain may not be able to discover each crew member's concerns, they must create an environment that they feel comfortable speaking up. To many, the captain or manager will be held in a level of esteem that junior ranks may think they cannot approach. This myth needs to be dispelled and if it remains, at least facilitates their immediate manager as a conduit in the first instance. For a co-pilot, the captain is that manager, so the relationship needs to be maintained accordingly.

Trustworthy.

Whether it be lives or livelihoods in the balance, in the end, the responsibility sits squarely with the captain. To successfully work with a team, they must trust their captain implicitly, but similarly, a captain must have trust in the crew.

One of the greatest frustrations of a co-pilot is when the captain endeavours to micro-manage the flight when it is the co-pilot's turn to fly the aircraft. The captain must trust the appropriately qualified pilot in the other seat and not continually interrupt and intervene. Equally, the captain must trust the cabin crew to carry out their duties. Nothing signals an underconfident or insecure leader than a constant need to provide unwarranted input.

A leader has to offer enough leeway for team members to not only perform their tasks but to push their boundaries and grow in a mentoring environment. And yes, even allow them to make mistakes – although not major ones. The learning that can be achieved through mistakes must never be underestimated.

Appearance and Punctuality....or do as I do.

The stereotype of an airline captain is straight off a recruiting poster. The square-jawed male with greying hair, the peak-cap pulled down to frame the face, golden wings on the chest and gold bars on the shoulder, striding through the airport terminal. For starters, let's lose the male imagery. In all honesty, there is not a stereotypical leader in appearance, gender, race or even style of leadership.

However, the appearance of the leader needs to convey their expectation of how their business is to be projected. In an airline, the uniform serves a functional purpose in that it immediately identifies who is in charge to both the crew and passengers. This is particularly critical in an emergency such as an evacuation when the captain's uniform can be seen as a rallying point for passengers and a point of contact for first responders.

In a more typical workplace, the leader's appearance and punctuality sets the standard for the staff and projects the company's image to clients. There will be outliers and workplaces where appearance is not critical, but generally, it is the first indicator a customer has to the professionalism of an individual. That glimpse of a pilot walking through a gate lounge to the aircraft may be the only interaction they have with their passengers. Regardless of their experience and qualifications, it is that fleeting glimpse of the crew that establishes the initial trust in their ability to navigate the skies safely.

Influential.

For all of these qualities, a captain is an influencer who can influence others, the situation and the outcome. Through a range of techniques, a captain will guide the aircraft and crew through what is a very dynamic operational environment. In doing so, a variety of personality types, environments and sometimes situations outside their control will need to be managed and, in normal operations, this is best achieved through guidance and trust. However, there will be times when the captain needs to raise the level of intensity and be more direct to achieve the outcome crisply in the timeframe available. It is this ability to exercise emotional intelligence and adapt to the situation as required that is pivotal in becoming a good captain.

Being a good captain is an ongoing journey, learning from each and every new situation and over time warding off complacency in that which seems routine. Recognising mistakes and addressing them honestly, while still being able to move forward. Leadership is a task in which you will never score 100 per cent correct, but the days that you get close are very satisfying.

PEOPLE

Why Good Co-Pilots Can Make Great Captains

"**G**ood Co-Pilots make Great Captains" can be interpreted in two ways - and that is intentional. In the first instance, the skills learnt as a co-pilot by observing a range of captains, plays a significant role in forming the captain that a pilot will ultimately become. Equally, a great captain is often made so by possessing the awareness and humility to employ the skill-set of the supporting co-pilot. These same traits apply to all forms of leadership and management that exist beyond the confines of the cockpit.

The leadership skills, ego and processes that constitute a successful captain or manager are the constant undercurrent within this book. However, the skills in being a good co-pilot come with their challenges but ultimately create a better leader in the long term. A captain that has been rapidly promoted in an expanding airline may have limited exposure to the life and challenges in the role of a subordinate. Very quickly, they have become the "boss", and their management style becomes the norm. Human factors training, humility and emotional intelligence are key to improving in this case. Recognising that fate has dealt a kind hand for a rapid rise through the ranks and that it does not necessarily constitute an extensive foundation is the first step. Checking the ego and continuing to look, listen and learn from others is the best way to consolidate the position.

Conversely, a co-pilot that has spent several years in the subordinate role, has seen all types of captains – the good, bad and the ugly. The master operators and the impetuous tyrants, the intellectuals and those that struggle. The cool under pressure and the not so cool at any time. Each flight and each captain contribute a little more to the tapestry that will ultimately constitute the fabric of the co-pilot's own command style when the time comes. When a new co-pilot emerges from the simulator, they can usually fly the aircraft with incredible precision. To be endorsed to fly the aircraft, their ability has been tested under a range of difficult circumstances. However, it is their skills in monitoring and support that truly constitute their new role.

Even though not actively flying the aircraft, there exists a responsibility to continually observe and cross-check the operation. The duty extends far beyond simply being told what to do. It calls for active mental participation in considering the aircraft's flight path, what comes next and how that will be achieved. When the other pilot's actions differ, the degree of monitoring is heightened to determine whether it is an error or a difference in technique. And if concern remains, it is time to raise those concerns by "managing upwards" as discussed elsewhere in this book.

Without thorough knowledge, the co-pilot is in danger of being little more than a passenger in a uniform. Only through a solid knowledge base can they recognise any digression from the norm or be equipped to challenge the captain with the appropriate degree of tact and if needed, propose an alternative.

A technique offered by some captains to assist their co-pilots is that of a "shared mental model". In this, the captain will not only relate the task ahead, but the style they plan to adopt to achieve this. Through this clarification, the co-pilot can monitor the shared mental model, rather than having a lurking question arising from the captain's technique. This uncertainty, no matter how slight, can be a distraction and detract from the task of monitoring.

Good captains also offer their co-pilots the opportunity to operate the aircraft as if they were in command. They allow them to make decisions, communicate with the company and the cabin crew. They will enable them to make judgements regarding the weather ahead or the altitude at which to fly—all the while nurturing their experience, building confidence and mentoring them for their future role.

There will also be days spent flying with captains that may not have such a nurturing nature and these are the days that make good co-pilots even better. Despite any level of tension or disharmony, the task must prevail as the priority. If communication is a challenge, then sitting silently is not the answer. Check the ego, raise your own game and go above and beyond to support the captain.

Use the C.A.I.R language to elevate concerns if needed and always initially suggest options with tact unless safety is in the balance and time is of the essence. In most situations, a lack of tact is the quickest way to become further alienated and increase the degree of difficulty. By contrast, phrasing a query with "I" may seem to place the failing on the supporting pilot, but it can often be the quickest and easiest means to a resolution. "I may be wrong, but…", "I haven't done this before, but shouldn't we…", "I understand that to mean…"

The time spent as a subordinate, a co-pilot, may at times have levels of frustration, but these are learning opportunities. Why was that captain so annoying? Why didn't that captain understand? Why did he do that? Why, why, why? A good co-pilot will review these situations and consider other options. They will also remember why, as a co-pilot, it was an unpleasant experience and tailor their behaviour when they attain command.

In any organisation, the path to a senior role is often a long road. Rather than allowing frustration and envy to surface, treat every experience, good and bad, as part of the apprenticeship. Withdrawing support and being bitter or confrontational will not expedite the journey. Taking it all on board, volunteering for the less desirable tasks and maintaining calm in the face of increasing pressure are the qualities that will draw positive attention. Even the harshest manager will find it challenging to degrade a subordinate when the junior rank is not just doing their job - but doing more.

It is essential to treat the time as a co-pilot as a critical role, no matter how long the rise to command may take. The passengers' safe conveyance is the goal, and that cannot be compromised by any crew member's impatience or frustration. Good co-pilots treat every day as an opportunity to raise their standards and do better than the day before. Armed with this attitude and the correct skills is the reason that good co-pilots can make even greater captains.

PEOPLE

Put Your Oxygen On First

We have all sat through the safety demonstration in the passenger cabin of an airliner. In the case of a loss of cabin pressure, the masks will drop from the ceiling. However, rather than the age-old adage of "Women and children first", the presentation instructs you to put your oxygen on first. Why? Because at that moment you are the most important person and without that action, you will be of no use to anyone.

Without oxygen, humans are susceptible to a state of hypoxia – a lack of oxygen at "call level". In the first instance, slow-onset may result in confusion, tingling in the lips and fingers and vision fading to black and white. Ultimately, a state of unconsciousness may occur. That unconscious state will have a rapid onset should an aircraft lose cabin pressure at high altitude, where the atmosphere is thin, and less oxygen is available. The aircraft may lose its pressurisation system, possibly due to a system failure, or more dramatically, a sizeable hole in the skin of the aircraft. That's why the priority is to fit the mask and start the oxygen flowing.

Pilots refer to the "Time of Useful Consciousness". In their language, that equates to how long they have without sufficient oxygen before their mental process, and physical co-ordination is eroded to the level that they cannot fit their oxygen mask. At 35,000 feet, a typical altitude at which most airliners fly, this timeframe could be 30 seconds, or even less. That is 30 seconds to realise that something is wrong, stay calm and fit an oxygen mask. Fortunately, pilots are regularly trained in a flight simulator to do this and then descend to the aircraft to a lower altitude where the air is richer in oxygen. They are also aided by masks that are close at hand and designed to be fitted quickly.

There have been high-profile accidents where aircraft, their passengers and crew have been tragically lost due to the effects of hypoxia. In 1999, famed US professional golfer, Payne Stewart, was lost on board a corporate jet and in 2005, a Boeing 737 Greek airliner was lost. In both cases, military fighter jets were scrambled to intercept the aircraft, only to find crew slumped at the controls, or the windscreen iced over on the inside. Interestingly, the fighter pilots that intercepted the airliner did briefly see someone in the cockpit wave at them. It was found to be a flight attendant who had fitted a portable oxygen mask but who was unable to fly the aircraft. Its engines went silent as it ran out of fuel shortly after the sighting.

Consequently, the single act of fitting one's oxygen mask first is critical.

On the flight deck, once oxygen is flowing to the pilots, they can take the necessary actions to manoeuvre the aircraft to safety. In the cabin, once they are receiving oxygen, parents can then fit the masks to their children who may not be able to achieve this on their own. For the greater good, the individual's first action needs to be a selfish one. And this is true in other aspects of life and leadership roles.

A manager can only effectively undertake their wide range of duties if they are physically capable of doing so. This calls for adequate rest, exercise, and nutrition to keep fatigue and illness at bay. Ongoing education to stay at the leading edge of their field and continued self-improvement. Leisure time with family and friends is also important.

Just as ignoring everyone else until one's own oxygen is fitted; it may seem counter-intuitive to be focussed on oneself as the essential element when there is a greater responsibility in play. However, to fulfil those responsibilities effectively, a leader must be physically, mentally, and emotionally competent.

There will always be those that are driven to extremes, working incredible hours, and ignoring their own needs for the sake of the business. However, this management style also has a limit; it has its own "Time of Useful Consciousness." It may not be measured in seconds, but it is there, and like hypoxia depriving the body's cells of oxygen, the initial onset may be slow and insidious. At first, the manager's "aircraft" may be silently leaking oxygen without the drama of a window blowing out of the airframe in the first instance. Fatigue, confusion, missed appointments and opportunities may creep into their world without them even noticing.

They may feel that the success of the business and the livelihoods of others depends upon their selfless commitment. To a degree, this commitment is needed but "burn out" may be just around the corner, and when this occurs, the organisation cannot help but suffer. Even at this stage, all is not lost.

While the onset of hypoxia may not be evident to an individual, it may be apparent to those around them who have fitted their own masks. Another benefit of an open, honest culture within an organisation is that others can openly communicate without fear of retribution. It is the culture promoted on flight decks and is equally valuable in any workplace. Junior managers need to feel free to approach their managers when they recognise the symptoms of corporate hypoxia. They can offer to fit their colleague's "oxygen mask" by unburdening them of workload and encouraging them to take respite.

At times corporate culture suggests that working 20-hour days is the path to success, but it is an effort that cannot be sustained. Pilots have legally regulated maximum flight and duty times and minimum rest periods to ensure that they can perform at peak performance. It also facilitates an adequate reserve of mental capacity to cope with various stresses such as bad weather or an inflight emergency. On the surface, it may seem profitable to squeeze more flying hours out of a pilot, but with the degradation of performance comes an increased chance of an accident. No-one wants to be a passenger on that airliner.

A leader taking care of themselves is not a selfish act – it is a necessary strategy for being competent and able to execute their duties to the best of their ability. In doing so, the organisation benefits from sound leadership with reserves of energy to deal with the unexpected. It is critical to success that as a leader, you put your oxygen on first.

PEOPLE

Check Your Ego

It is often said in aviation that when you think you know it all, you are dangerous. Flight itself is not inherently dangerous, but it can be brutally unforgiving and cracking the door open to complacency is an invitation to fate. Other than being a successful military recruiting tool and good fun to watch, the movie "Top Gun" in many ways displayed the qualities that were the antithesis of the professional pilot – mainly when it came to ego.

A professional in any field should be confident, but that confidence stems from a sound foundation of knowledge and experience – not false bravado. Arrogance and a bristling ego can be the defence mechanisms of those that lack the necessary qualities. Like a termite-ridden shack that's given a shining coat of paint, it may look great, but you do not have to push too hard to realise that there is nothing underneath.

The issue is not that these individuals are annoyingly the loudest person at every party – it's more serious than that. Their behaviour negatively impacts communication, decision-making, planning and a raft of other processes. Processes that could result in improved efficiency and safety if they checked their ego and encouraged others to participate.

A subdued ego is not a sign of weakness; instead, it is an indicator of quiet self-confidence. Admitting mistakes is not a sign of incompetence; it reinforces that no-one is infallible and that the first step to any solution or degree of improvement is identifying the problem.

Displaying humility will earn respect from colleagues and subordinates alike. It will also open the channels of communication, inviting feedback from the entire team. Arrogance will discourage this behaviour, either from fear of ridicule, retribution or being ignored. Some will even take pleasure in remaining silent, allowing the offender to fail openly. And herein lies the issue – the task suffers.

A flight crew's goal is to safely and efficiently convey their passengers to their destination. It is not about point-scoring as one pilot watches the other fail or demonstrating superior prowess over another. It is about operating as a team to achieve the goal, and this applies equally in business.

As a leader, it is important not to be dismissive. Always listen to others and be genuinely attentive as their suggestion may be worthwhile, and even when it isn't, it is an opportunity for learning. The simple act of pausing and listening to a more junior employee raises their spirits, self-respect and encourages future input.

In the flight deck environment, typically a captain and co-pilot may fly "leg for leg", meaning that they will alternate between being the pilot actually flying the sector and operating in a support role. That is, one takes-off, flies and lands, while the other monitors the operation, takes responsibility for radio transmissions, flight logs, etc., etc. It is an essential technique as it not only shares the load, but it offers each crew member firsthand insight into both roles regularly. For the co-pilot, it is an opportunity to operate the aircraft as if they are in command and the best captains make the most of this opportunity. And they do so by shelving their ego.

In this scenario, a co-pilot may suggest an alternative way of planning an arrival, or possibly suggest the carriage of more fuel than the captain may think necessary. As a captain and a leader, it's important to take the plan on board and if it isn't too far from the mark, allow the plan to go ahead. Interfering and imposing one's plan doesn't offer the opportunity to learn. If there is a shortfall in the co-pilot's strategy, it will be more effectively reinforced through execution than being overruled beforehand. Additionally, more than one captain has learnt a valuable lesson from a co-pilot, by shelving their ego.

The junior party can also be guilty of ego – it is not an elite club. If it's a case of over-confidence, then the tasks set for the co-pilot or employee can increase in their challenge until a degree of humility is drawn out naturally. This should not be an "I told you so" moment for a captain or manager, rather a technique to draw out the best through the subordinate reaching the realisation on their own.

Another far from desirable situation that can occur when the co-pilot's ego gets in the way is known as "withdrawing support". This may initially have been provoked by an over-zealous captain or some other issue that offended the co-pilot; however, the flight deck is not the place for escalation. In the case of "withdrawing support", the offending co-pilot doesn't interfere with the operation; they just fail to support the captain. And in instances when they should draw oversights to the captain's attention, they remain silent with a smug "let them work it out" attitude. It is an exceedingly rare and dangerous situation and if detected, must be addressed as soon as possible. The first indicator is a reduced level of verbal input other than what is necessary. As in any relationship, faltering communication can be a "red flag" for a greater underlying issue. A leader's job is to encourage feedback both good and bad. The absence of any feedback can be an indicator by stealth that the communication and the relationship are breaking down with the task ultimately suffering.

There is no room for exercising an ego in the workplace. It raises unseen barriers where the constant transfer of information and respect should take place. It can escalate a situation when egos collide or subdue one party when an imbalance exists. Neither situation is the best for the overriding priority of completing the task and achieving the goal, and it will always be greater than any one individual.

PEOPLE

Check Your Emotions

We are all different, and the ability to "check our emotions" can be more easily achieved by some. In the airline industry, when recruiting pilots, a company will often profile candidates psychologically. Qualities such as being an analytical thinker, self-controlled and not impulsive, tend to be common to those lists. In the potential crucible of an emergency when the sights and sounds of the situation tear at the human response to panic, a pilot is trained to proceed logically – to adhere to the process, think clearly and check their emotions. Not all professions reach such training.

Beyond the recruitment process, a key element is the training of pilots for emergencies in advance, thus exposing them to that crucible by replicating environment. In a flight simulator, the flashing lights and ringing bells, even the sound of rushing air, can be recreated. The simulator can shudder and shake, all the while the crew will be expected to fly the aircraft and follow their process. They strive to maintain a rhythm, a cadence, in the face of the chaos. By doing so, they avoid rushing, acting on impulse and can process the situation as it continues to evolve.

Not all fields of endeavour come with their own flight simulator. However, most are not called upon to potentially operate in such extreme circumstances. Even so, there is the ability to consider our emotions in advance of them surfacing at an inopportune time.

In several instances, we can recognise in advance an environment that may provoke us emotionally. It may be a setting, a work environment, or an individual. Feelings of trepidation can manifest as false bravado or anger, and ongoing frustration can build up and result in lashing out.

Our best defence can be recognising the physiological responses in ourselves, such as an increased breathing rate, sweating, speech becoming quicker and possibly louder. We may have personal traits such as folding our arms or putting our hands on our hips.

Conversely, stepping back, slowing breathing and consciously slowing speech can have both a calming effect and give an outward appearance of calm. Even if on the inside, there is a small wrestling match taking place. Knowing our bodies and tendencies can assist in circumventing an emotional response. Unlike flight deck operations, there may even be the option of temporarily and politely excusing oneself from the situation until thoughts and composure can be regrouped.

There will be occasions when the temptation exists to follow a "gut feeling", but this should not be confused with an irrational, emotional response. A "gut feeling", or intuition, is the brain calling upon past experiences and comparing them to the current situation. That conflict between intuition and a plan is not the trigger to abandon a plan but a healthy indicator to revisit the plan and review it. If this is done collaboratively with the team or crew, another member may be able to provide input to solidify the intuition into an aspect of the plan.

In any situation, the importance of maintaining composure in a leadership role cannot be understated. Aside from allowing the brain to process information and make decisions with clarity, irrational outbursts undermine respect and confidence in the leader.

Furthermore, the moment discussions erode into phrases such as "Just do it!", or "Because I said so!", the instruction has become the will of one person, closed off to feedback. Those called upon to complete the task lack any ownership and the level of care falls away.

And having been barked at and not listened to, fellow employees are highly unlikely to return and offer the ever-valuable feedback that is critical to future improvement. The task suffers, and the safe and efficient completion of the task is the goal that stands above any personality.

If the emotions still rise up and irrationally take over the process or the difference of opinion, then *retreat, recognise the fact and check the ego*. Calm down and take ownership of the situation, even if it may feel as if it was provoked by another. Be a leader, apologise and set the standard straight in a calm and composed manner.

When the immediate situation has been resolved, it is again time to step back and sit in the "jumpseat" to take in the bigger picture. Was this an isolated incident? Is there an underlying cause? Fatigue, family stress and work pressures can build up and sometimes it is an outburst that is the first indicator of a limit being reached. In the same way that an aircraft accident can be attributed to multiple causal factors and "holes in the Swiss Cheese", it is rarely "pilot error" alone. To prevent a repeat in the future, the underlying issues need to be addressed.

As with any aspect of aviation, being prepared in advance and early recognition of a problem is an integral strategy. Our emotions may not be as well defined as the failure of a physical component at a critical moment of flight; however, the impact can be just as great if not addressed.

PEOPLE

CRM.
Crew Resource Management

Crew Resource Management, or CRM, was originally known in some quarters as Cockpit Resource Management. To limit this management technique to the cockpit was at odds with the very concept that recognises a range of resources exist beyond the flight deck door. In fact, the principles are applicable to any organisation.

CRM is the effective use of *all available resources* to achieve safe and efficient operations by utilising good communication, reducing error, and avoiding stress. It is the emphasis on "all available resources" that emerged as the revolutionary concept in the airline industry when CRM became universally respected decades ago.

Up to that point, the airline captain had been perceived as the ultimate answer to all of the problems. Born of lone wolf aviation pioneers and followed by a generation of wartime pilots, the image and reality were of the stoic, solo leader. However, as the airline industry delved further in the pursuit of safety, it found that such strength could also be a weakness. Ego and attitude could alienate those around them, and the degree of self-belief and ego would prevent the commander seeking help. It was a situation that was exacerbated by the awe in which the unchallenged position of airline captain was held. Even though airline captains are human - and humans make mistakes.

The problem was further emphasised by a spate of accidents in the 1970s. Despite ever-improving aircraft technology, devastating airline accidents continued to occur, Troublingly, aircraft were being lost in seemingly preventable accidents, the crew often distracted by another, smaller issue – as small as a blown bulb in one instance.

The hierarchical heritage of the captain was failing. The aircraft had grown too complex to draft a procedure for every contingency and for any one pilot to manage alone. Events had to be better managed, using every available resource that is at hand. In a world that was once perceived as black and white, the "soft skills" of communication, emotional intelligence, and decision-making became vital. They did not replace checklists and processes but modified the way in which they were managed.

Additionally, not every eventuality can be anticipated with a checklist or mitigated against in advance. CRM gave crews new skills that allowed them to adapt in these situations more readily. Through effectively exchanging information and permitting the captain to operate *within* the team, as opposed to towering over it, the ability to respond to the unforeseen was greatly enhanced.

CRM was introduced, and training often highlighted the human shortcomings in these accidents. Around this was built a training system that encouraged a less dictatorial regime in favour of a more consultative process. This did not erode the captain's final authority as pilot-in-command but enhanced the processes that were used to exercise that authority. The change in behaviour did not occur overnight, and in certain parts of the world, social cultures still propagate the myth of the captain almighty. Fortunately, for the greater proportion of world airline operations, CRM has been embraced and embedded within the company culture.

CRM ties together many of the techniques, tactics and strategies that we have already discussed. It calls for checking the ego and exercising humility and respecting peers and subordinates alike for their skill set, making decisions by drawing information from every available channel and considering feedback. Importantly, it creates an environment where open communication can flow in both directions.

Of all the elements of a company's culture and flight deck strategy that allow CRM to reduce errors and improve efficiency, open and honest communication is paramount. Laying the foundations for this occur from the moment pilots first meet in the crew room before the flight and that first encounter is critically important. A warm, professional welcome by the captain to the crew and a relaxed discussion, often non-aviation related can put their crew at ease and set the mood. This is no different, be it in the briefing room or the boardroom. First impressions matter as they set the tone.

It is worth remembering once again that two pilots may have never met before, be of different generations, gender and social outlook. And yet, within an hour, they can be jointly focused on a standard task and a common goal. This is the strength of CRM and company culture as it exists in successful and safe airlines.

In drawing together all available resources, a captain will reach far beyond their co-pilot. Depending on the task at hand, they will call upon flight attendants, flight planning staff, ground personnel, refuellers, engineers, the operations centre and more, tying together what each party has to offer. This is done successfully through polite and professional behaviour towards every individual within the operation. It has been said that the key to exercising sound CRM skills are basically "common sense and good manners."

A potential threat to leaders is that in pulling together so many elements, the situation can become confused. CRM encourages delegation to responsible parties with a direct instruction to report back. Whether managing an inflight situation or striving for a departure in the wake of a ground-based problem, captain's will frequently start to keep a simple log of the process with a time noted for when an event occurred or a duty was delegated. This maintains a real perception of time as this can be lost amid multi-tasking under pressure.

Additionally, a short log tracks the roles that have been delegated and the tasks yet to be completed. Only when that log has been completed, is the situation truly resolved and even then, a quick review and asking the team, "Have we covered everything?" further confirms that all matters have been addressed.

This simple log of events also serves another vital purpose. In the subsequent review of an event, details have been captured and are of particular use if reporting is required. It may also highlight a step that has been missed that can be noted for future management challenges. Furthermore, the log will outline those people in the process that need to be thanked or further recognised. Sometimes in the heat of the moment, this courtesy can be overlooked, however praise and recognition for a job well done is essential for the continued success of the team and the tasks ahead.

Crew Resource Management is an inclusive management technique that can be bred and strengthened through a company's culture and training. It can be exercised through mundane tasks and critical incidents alike. There will always be the need for the ultimate responsibility to rest with a captain or manager, however, by practising sound CRM, those outcomes will be reached by a far more complete means than any one individual can achieve on their own.

PEOPLE

Cockpit Gradient

Unfortunately, as we have all witnessed at some stage, promotion is not always based upon merit and talent. Politics, personalities and even nepotism can come into play. In the airline industry, promotion is often based upon "seniority", which stems from the date of joining that company. It does not consider what experience has transpired beforehand.

Consequently, a senior air force test pilot with 10,000 hours of flight time will join the airline at the bottom of the list and be "junior" to pilots with far less of a background in aviation. Transferring between airlines is also met with a slippery slide down the pole and can be likened to a doctor changing hospitals but having to commence their employment as a nurse's aide. This being said, every pilot is aware of how the system works and makes their career choices knowingly, with lifestyle overriding status on some occasions.

The flow-on effect to the flight deck can be the same as in a company's management, that the senior manager may be senior in experience, or they may not. It is a situation that needs to be managed with intelligence, maturity and humility by all parties as the safe and efficient execution of the flight, or task, must remain the priority.

On the flight deck, the term "cockpit gradient" refers to the hierarchy in decision-making and the ultimate power of command, whether actual or perceived. In all cases, if mismanaged, it can harm the operation and ultimately endanger the aircraft and all on board. A core purpose of "Crew Resource Management" was to educate crews about cockpit gradient and to recognise potentially unsafe gradients.

Also referred to as an "authority gradient", it ideally needs to run from the senior party "downhill" and with the correct slope in most instances. Too steep from a domineering captain downwards and two-way communication is hampered, inhibiting valuable input and feedback from the co-pilot. If the gradient is flat, command decisions may be delayed or overlooked, and the door is open to procrastination as both parties either defer to the other or are too "polite" and hesitant to raise issues with the other. In other cases, the gradient can reverse, and the junior partner exerts undue influence upon a weaker captain. In all of these scenarios, communication is hampered, decision-making is compromised, and the operation is disadvantaged.

Cockpit gradient was cited as a contributing factor in the worst accident in aviation history, when two Boeing 747s collided on the runway at Tenerife in 1977, killing more than 300 people. The investigation found that the KLM Boeing 747 had taken off in low visibility without an Air Traffic Control clearance while a Pan Am 747 was still on the runway. The captain of the KLM 747 was the airline's chief flying instructor and had even featured in one of the airline's advertising campaigns. Such was his status, that even though the rest of the crew initially raised doubt regarding the lack of clearance, they did not fully assert their concerns. Consequently, the captain continued the take-off regardless of the uncertainty. The gradient was too steep, and as mentioned, CRM evolved from this accident, addressing the issue of authority gradient.

Ideally, the gradient has a slight slope down from the captain to their crew or the manager to their staff. Drawing the analogy of a see-saw, a ball is free to run downhill easily but can be pushed back uphill with minimal force. However, under the usual status quo, the ball will always run down from the captain.

CRM emphasises the importance of an airline's culture and individual crew's role in establishing the correct gradient through an environment that encourages open communication from all parties. In most cases, it will fall upon the captain to develop the balance through a warm but professional rapport, however, not always.

In some cases, the subordinate needs to exercise emotional intelligence and as we've said elsewhere in this book, check one's ego. In the case where the 10,000-hour air force test pilot is flying as the co-pilot to a less experienced captain, the correct cockpit gradient can be aided by the co-pilot taking the initiative. Even using language such as, "Would you like this radio tuned?", or "Is it a suitable time for me to walk around the aircraft and conduct the external inspection now?". They may be everyday duties that the co-pilot can easily conduct without oversight, subtle deference can establish a suitable authority gradient when, at first glance, the experience levels may suggest it should slope the other way. Humility is a valuable tool on the flight deck, with the task always taking priority over the individual.

Possessing a gentle gradient in the correct direction in no way undermines the captain's ultimate authority as the pilot-in-command. To the contrary, it is a means of garnering respect when a captain invites the entire crew to be a part of the process. Rather than appearing threatened by the experience of another crew member, they identify it as a resource. Generally, the crew member will respond enthusiastically and cohesion will occupy the space that could have so easily have been filled by conflict.

Whether it is a cockpit gradient on a flight deck, or an authority gradient in another form of organisation, recognising defined roles and individual experience for their respective benefits will lead to a safer and more efficient outcome. The captain will always have the final authority, but that will be based upon mutual respect and management skills, not the title associated with the position.

PEOPLE

TEAMWORK

A irline operations call for a small team of potential strangers, to meet and establish a rapport within an hour before being confined inside flight deck for hours upon end. All the while, they are tasked with safely guiding one of humankind's most complex craft at near the speed of sound, through a hostile sub-zero environment starved of oxygen. How do they function? Teamwork.

Far from having the boss seated at the head of the table, even the ergonomics of the flight deck are in line with equity and a beneficial cockpit gradient. Both pilots sit side-by-side, each with the ability to reach every switch on the flight deck needed to operate the aircraft. Roles can be reversed, information easily shared, flight instruments and systems readily observed from either pilot's seat. The design is tailor-made for a team to operate effectively.

Despite the captain ultimately being in command, a flight crew is able to derive the best outcomes through not relying on an individual. Nor is the process solely one-way and from the "top-down". There remains a positive authority gradient from the captain, but there will be occasions when the best solutions are offered by the lower ranks.

The saying that "two heads are better than one" is never truer than on the flight deck. It is a truism proved time and again and can even be seen in the digital world. Networking a series of computers will always have more capacity than a room full of independent units.

The flight deck also draws technology into the team. Flight Management Computers, or FMCs, are the aircraft's brain. Each pilot has a keyboard and screen adjacent to their knee through which data can be entered, calculations made, and plans executed. The information provided by this additional team member can prove vital but must always be treated with a critical eye. Its calculations are based upon the human input, so an error at the front end can result in a blow out at the back end.

This is managed by a simple process of cross-checking. No data is executed without firstly being positively cross-checked and confirmed by another crew member. Technology has enhanced aviation safety, although the crew have needed to learn how to integrate the new team member. It can be a major cause of task saturation. And even when not "saturated", the crew will often brief that they are going "head down" to make entries into the FMC. This alerts the other pilot of their current focus and alerts them to manage the flight path. Both pilots should never both be "heads down".

However, building a team, is not always a straightforward task as there can be a wide range of dynamics and personalities involved. These personalities have been formed over the years, based on family, culture, upbringing, social environment and other factors that cannot be tailored to through a 60-minute briefing. What the crew do share is their task focus and professional pride, and this is a strong foundation for the workplace.

That workplace also has a tremendous role to play in the effectiveness of its teams. It can establish the company culture and define its processes and parameters for all to see, share and understand. The company can establish a baseline. Additionally, by utilising a common framework when addressing issues and tasks, it is effectively implementing Standard Operating Procedures, even if the SOPs are not as rigidly defined as they need to be for airline operations. They are creating an expectation of how the job gets done and offer the opportunity to highlight any divergence.

At the individual, operational level, common courtesy can go a long way in team building. Three "Ps" can be an important starting point to build rapport and avoid conflict.

P – Punctual.

P – Professional.

P – Polite.

It may seem obvious, but those disregarding these three behaviours have set in motion a poor crew dynamic on more than one occasion. There have even been situations where crew members have scored three from three in turning up late in an unkempt uniform without an excuse or apology. Fortunately, this is a rare occurrence.

What is more frustrating is that they are simple Ps to which one can adhere. From a captain's perspective, they offer an air of keenness, responsibility, and respect. When observed in a captain, they generate the same sentiments but importantly, quickly create a professional setting that corresponds to the company culture and invites open communication.

Punctuality also removes the element of time compression, which can create stress in a work environment and even avail time for non-operational discussions which can enhance relationships. Being professional extends beyond grooming and general appearance, although that is important, and we all know the saying about first impressions counting. Professionalism includes being fit to operate, well versed in the information that is to be discussed and active in any discussions. Being polite should be an implicit prerequisite.

Added to the challenge of team building is that crews may be called upon to operate on close quarters with people that as individuals they may not like. It may not be anything, in particular, just a contrast in personalities. In these situations, particularly for a subordinate, the "Three Ps" are essential – there is no point looking for conflict which may easily have been avoided.

Tension in a workplace, particularly a flight deck, can adversely affect productivity, or worse, safety. The symptoms of the tension will not always be obvious. It may manifest in long periods of silence, an unwillingness to maintain eye contact in discussion or a reluctance to contribute anything above the basic level required. Rather than escalating the situation, check the ego, and offer to assist by undertaking an extra or undesirable duty. Despite the temptation, do not reflect the behaviour with additional silence or reduced input. Place the task first – it's larger than any team.

Another point of note that applies not infrequently to flight crews is that the technical nature of aviation can appeal to a particular character type. These pilots are often fantastic operational people with a deep and thorough knowledge but are not as comfortable with interpersonal skills. This slight awkwardness is often shyness but can be misinterpreted as aloofness when that is certainly not the case. Making an effort to find common ground with these workmates is often appreciated more than one can understand.

Seeking common, neutral ground for non-operational discussions is a safe haven, however if an operational issue needs to be raised in a strained environment, use the C.A.I.R. language described in "Managing Upwards" to escalate the concern in a tactful way smoothly. Bearing in mind, if the operation is in danger of being negatively impacted, the task always remains the priority. When reminded of that, even the most belligerent team member will generally reluctantly comply.

Should the organisation involve out of hours social interactions, such as crew overnighting away from home, it is important to observe still the "Three Ps" in the company of the team. An unfortunate "out of hours" incident, even if isolated, can severely damage the rapport between the crew. If of a nature beyond the normal workplace guidelines, the ramifications may be far greater.

It may seem strange that such a simple, almost childish strategy needs to be discussed at such a level. However, history has proven that even these common graces cannot be taken for granted at times. The workplace can call unlike personalities to perform complex tasks under pressure. To achieve success, it is advantageous to commence from a sound baseline established by a company's cultures and processes and the individual's common courtesy.

PEOPLE

MAKING MISTAKES

No human, machine or organisation is infallible – particularly humans. An entire branch of aviation studies is dedicated to "Human Factors" and taught to pilots from a very early stage and reinforced regularly in airline classrooms around the world. Psychology, physiology, the human-technology interface and operating under stress are just some of the areas of study. Still, mistakes can never be eradicated, but their prevention, management and review can play a significant role in minimising their impact.

We tend to learn more from our mistakes than we do from our successes. Mistakes highlight our shortcomings and challenge us to do better. In contrast, success does not automatically create a need for learning and can, in fact, open the way for weaknesses such as complacency. The environment in which mistakes are made and subsequently addressed again stems back to the culture of an organisation.

A mistake is not a reckless act beyond the recognised limits, rogue behaviour or a malicious deed. It may be misjudged or even misguided, but its nature is such that positives can be gained from the experience and improvements made.

It is said, "good decisions come from experience, but experience comes from bad decisions". This truism recognises that a "just culture" seeks to learn rather than punish or ignore a mistake and stands to reap the benefits of the knowledge gained through unplanned and unfortunate means. Combined with a healthy culture of reporting, a mistake can be further examined to reveal an isolated incident, or possibly an organisation-wide trend—the subsequent response to each varying in nature.

The first strategy to employ is to safeguard against mistakes. Addressed throughout this book is the concept of reducing hazards through pre-defined parameters, open communication, and processes are all safeguards that can be put in place. They are designed to either prevent a mistake occurring or provide triggers for when a situation is straying from the normal realm of operation, generating a resolution.

Mistakes can be made at any time, but the implementation of new equipment, new personnel or training are all reasons for increased vigilance as the relevant experience will not have yet been gained. In a training situation, an experienced instructor may well identify a looming error and even let it evolve to a degree as part of the learning process. If it's a minor administrative oversight, it may be allowed to occur in full to demonstrate both the mistake and the means of rectification thoroughly. Drawing the positives from a potential negative is a cornerstone of training.

When a mistake has been identified and needs to be addressed, the response must be proportionate and delivered in a measured fashion. If an individual is being counselled, it needs to be done with tact and positivity and calmly to gain the maximum benefit. A supporting explanation and offering the reasons behind the need for additional training allows the individual to be a part of the process and not a target. The technique can be further enhanced through the humility of the trainer and management in accepting ownership. Perhaps recognising that the training was not consistent, or insufficient time was allocated and sharing that the organisation also stands to learn from the mistake.

When the mistake is made by a superior and needs to be addressed, the techniques expressed in the section on "Managing Upwards" can come into play. It is important not to ignore the mistake, but it needs to be raised with tact and without undermining the manager's position or potentially fragile ego. Again, taking ownership can play a vital role. Language such as, "I probably should have seen this earlier…", or, "I needed to give you better support..", serves to recognise the mistake and open the way for rectification and learning with all parties still engaged.

Reporting a mistake is the next stage in the process. An organisation must have a system in place that facilitates the reporting of mistakes of any significance, by any person, at any level. Often those on the lowest level of the organisational chart are best positioned to see a mistake manifest. In contrast, those in the boardroom may not see the after-effect for some time, by which stage it may have escalated.

Furthermore, a mistake in isolation may seem insignificant and only through an organised system can it be realised that a systemic fault exists and that the mistake is far from an isolated instance. Armed with valid information from reports, the mistake can be rectified, and processes, dissemination and training can take place to prevent a recurrence. Early identification of mistakes can be of immense value to an organisation, so creating a culture to encourage it and a system to support it should remain a priority.

To err is most definitely human, and we will continue to make mistakes as a part of our progress. Recognising that a genuine mistake is not a failing to be punished, but an opportunity to learn and improve will aid substantially in the mindset with which we address our mistakes and provide for better outcomes. And in turn, a better and more efficient organisation.

PEOPLE

Groundhog Day

It is said that aviation is hours of boredom interrupted by moments of sheer terror. However, all too often, the genuine threat can be found lurking in the boredom. A strictly procedural environment, on one type of aircraft, possibly over one or two air routes, can create a perception of "Groundhog Day", or "Same thing – Different day". However, thinking like this can crack the door for complacency to slip in and organise a moment of terror.

With repetition comes increased risk. The very act of doing something over and over may initially improve performance at a great rate, but beyond that, the maintenance of a standard requires a substantial effort. Lowered levels of vigilance, a temptation to take a short cut, decreased attention and lowered situational awareness can all occur when an endeavour becomes seemingly "too routine". When this becomes the status quo, the development of looming problems may initially go unnoticed.

It is not untoward to have a pilot who has flown 10,000 hours on one type of aircraft, and naturally, they can become remarkably familiar with their environment. However, for the passengers entrusting their lives to the crew, they do not know this or necessarily care. Like a show on the night of its 400th performance, it is still opening night for the audience, and they deserve the same level of commitment from the actors.

The first step toward prevention is recognition. When experience and surroundings have become the norm, a level of comfort can pervade when vigilance is what is needed. A pilot or manager needs to recognise this in themselves and their team. It may seem counterintuitive, but there is a need to double-down on the basics and the processes at this time, although the temptation may be to bypass them. Slowing down a process, backtracking to an earlier point if concentration is lost, or asking for an instruction to be repeated slowly no matter the level of experience, or how many times it's been done before. Through returning to core tasks and core values, the most robust "safety net" can be achieved. It only takes one variation on a well-practised routine to leave the entire operation and goal vulnerable.

Team members can remind each other that familiarity is a threat, and often, working with friends can present more threats than working with an adversary. Unless vigilant, the comfort factor of working with a friend can lead to certain safeguards being lowered and tasks being taken for granted. For some, it can also hamper the ability to be critical and raise concerns. Conversely, working with an adversary encourages a focus on the task and the safeguards are well and truly raised, almost waiting for an error that can be criticised. This is not a healthy attitude either and needs to be moderated. However, the heightened level of vigilance will tend to trap issues early on in the process.

Accordingly, when we work with friends, it's important to raise that point from the outset and reinforce that these are the days we might let our guard down. It is time to put the "game face" on and to take the initiative to encourage input and criticism. The environment can still be cordial, but it must always be professional.

Pilots can be assisted to retain their focus and passion if they have an interest away from the flight deck, just as friendships can be pursued and enjoyed outside the confines of the workplace.

The benefit of repetition rests with the individual. It can be used as a crutch to underpin a reduced level of effort, or it can be applied to further build a framework that expands situational awareness. When attention to detail remains in even the most mundane task, the detection of rising threats is aided. Whether at altitude or in an organisation, early detection can offer an advantage of time to rectify and reduce the scale of the impact.

"Groundhog Day" is the ally of complacency and complacency is the enemy of safe and efficient operations. As they say, "When you think you know everything, that's when you're dangerous."

PEOPLE

The Danger Of Distractions

*A*viate. *Navigate. Communicate.* These well-worn words are carved into the brain of every aviator from their earliest flights. Broken down into even more natural language it means that the pilot should always 'FLY THE AEROPLANE FIRST AND FOREMOST'. All other aspects of flight management are of little or no value if the pilot ignores the fundamentals and keeps the aircraft flying safely and clear of hitting the terrain.

Once the safety of the aircraft is assured, the next step is to comprehend where it is and where it is going fully. Only when this has occurred is thought given to communicating the situation to other parties and possibly seeking external assistance. This simple adage is a great catchphrase in reminding us to prioritise and is equally applicable on the flight deck and in our day-to-day.

Without consciously reminding ourselves to aviate, navigate and communicate, we can easily become distracted. Furthermore, with every ounce of increasing workload, the temptation to attend to secondary tasks grows greater. It stems partly from the very human trait of wanting to "tick something off the list". To feel some sense of completion, even if it is a secondary task. Unfortunately, the time and effort this redirects away from the primary task may render any such effort pointless, if not detrimental.

Additionally, this secondary distraction may present challenges of its own, drawing upon our limited resources of capacity and time further down the "rabbit hole". By this stage, our "situational awareness" may be severely compromised if not altogether lost. We are now entering an area where recovery may not even be possible.

In 1972, the Boeing 747 "Jumbo Jet" was still relatively in its infancy as the dawn of massive wide-bodied airliners began to populate the skies. To this backdrop, loss of Eastern Air Lines Flight 401 was a tragedy that shocked the world. The aircraft was only a few months old and the crew were highly experienced and yet a single "25 cent" light bulb on the flight deck brought the aircraft down. The crew became distracted, all focussing on trying to change the burnt-out bulb which was proving to be uncooperative. With no-one "aviating" and watching the aircraft's flight path, it disengaged from the autopilot system and descended. Ten seconds before impact into the Florida Everglades, the cockpit voice recorder (CVR) captured the veteran captain asking, "Hey – What's happening here?"

The subsequent investigation led to significant changes in the field of "Human Factors", and even today, the accident is used in training to showcase the danger of distractions, among other valuable lessons.

Our high-paced world has brought with it new ways to divert our attention through the same devices that have meant to streamline our processes. As smartphones, iPads and other tablets have become a part of our armoury; they have also become distractions that can divert our valuable attention if we allow this to occur. We have seen how such behaviour has caused carnage on our roads and inattention to priorities within our business can prove commercially lethal.

The first step in managing distractions is awareness. Realising that the very technologies that can assist us also have the potential to harm is crucial. Yet, we should not solely focus on the new technologies as we consider awareness as many of our old threats are still lurking.

Considering how we may be challenged is key and recognising that at the most basic level, even hunger, fatigue, illness and one's personal life can all prove to distract at times.

Employees and peers can be prone to interrupting at inopportune moments and to the uninformed bystander, cutting them off can appear rude. However, if within an organisation, it has been emphasised through training and company culture that distractions can be detrimental, raising the issue will be less offensive and be a matter of mutual understanding. In a relatively firm example, an airline introduced that the term "Red Flag", be spoken when the level of distraction was rising. Immediately, both pilots recognised the term and refocussed. There was no offence taken.

Despite a high level of awareness and preparedness, distractions will always occur as one cannot have control over everything. Accordingly, it is essential to deal with distractions appropriately when they arise.

If possible, eliminate the distraction. If it is a non-essential function, remove it. Turn the cell phone off. Even if you choose to ignore it supposedly, its ringing is an interruption and a challenge to your primary task.

Interruptions are possibly the most frequent distraction. They can come from a wide range of sources, human and hardware. Regaining the flow, can sometimes be difficult and we have all had those, "Now, where was I?" moments. If this happens, on the flight deck, it is normal to restart a checklist from the beginning to eliminate the chance of an omission. Go back a couple of steps in the process. A business may not come with a checklist, so find a known point in the process that you can recall with clarity and start again. If it's a piece of communication, ask for it to be repeated. You are the manager, the leader, so you always determine the pace and the direction of proceedings.

When unforeseen and seemingly urgent distractions occur, and they will, it is essential to prioritise. To harp on an old favourite, aviate, navigate and communicate. Always keep your aircraft safe, first and foremost. When the distraction first occurs, consider, "Is this distraction critical?" If not, ignore it for the moment and return to it later.

If the distraction is critical, then it needs to be attended to promptly. Ensuring that other primary tasks are not ignored may mean delegation, just as a captain may hand over physical control of the aircraft to the co-pilot, to free up capacity to attend to the issue that has arisen. Attempting to manage every task single-handedly will lead to overwhelm and the "rabbit hole" then beckons.

Prioritisation is always critically important and stating the prime focus verbally can ensure that everyone is on the "same page". Additionally, reminding others to speak up if it appears that the prime task is being overlooked offers another safety net. If someone on Flight 401 had simply spoken up, the airliner might not have flown into the Everglades.

Equally, in these circumstances, a "mini brief" as described elsewhere, can be invaluable – with emphasis on "mini". This is not an invitation to go into full-blown communications. Simply, whether in a team or operating alone, periodically ask and answer three simple questions.

"What's the main problem?"
"Where are we at, now?"
"Where do we go from here?"

These questions provide a brief update, a level of reassurance and an invitation for others to raise concerns. If a concern is raised, consider if it is a concern or a distraction. Prioritise and manage.

Distractions are always with us. Their form may be changing in this digital world of multi-tasking, but they still present the same threat. As pilots and managers, we need to be the filter that traps the distractions and puts them in their place. We can begin with awareness, while some we can eliminate and some we may need to prioritise. The more that we can manage distractions before they escalate, the safer our journey will be.

We need to recognise them for what they are – distractions. They may be the forebear of a greater emergency, but in the first instance, we must always continue to fly the aircraft safely. Only when we are in a safe place, can we divert our attention to resolve, manage or dismiss the distraction. Always be the pilot-in-command of your task and never let a simple distraction develop into a disaster.

PEOPLE

SITUATIONAL AWARENESS – AND WHEN YOU LOSE IT

Have you ever been blocked in a supermarket aisle by a trolley while the shopper peers at a shelf? Or caught behind a car creeping along slowly in the overtaking lane? Maybe you have read about a tourist so focused on framing a "selfie" that they walked backwards and fell over a precipice. These are all examples of people who are not appreciating the world around them – they are not situationally aware.

Perhaps one of the most critical skills that a pilot must possess is "situational awareness". It is also one of the most valuable yet transferable skills to every other aspect of our lives. From driving a motor vehicle, to running a business. Put simply, it is constantly understanding, "Where am I? and Where am I going?" More broadly, this can only be achieved with an appreciation of the surrounding environment.

Pilots operate their aircraft in three dimensions and in a dynamic environment. They need to continually project their future position in time and space and assess the best means to achieve that. The aircraft may currently be at 38,000 feet and flying at 76% the speed of sound, but in twenty minutes it must cross the landing threshold of a runway at a much slower speed to land. Along the way, there may be weather to avoid and other aircraft to remain a safe distance upon, requiring a change in speed or direction. The aircraft will need to be slowed to a speed where the wing flaps can be extended, and the landing gear can be lowered. Only by considering all these factors can the goal of a safe landing be reached, and it is a constant process of assessment and judgement.

In driving a car, we may anticipate a stop sign, but in being situationally aware we may appreciate that the car's brakes are due for service, there is oil on the road, and a child is playing with a ball on the footpath nearby. Situational awareness is an appreciation of *all* factors affecting our current circumstances and what may lie ahead.

It may appear an obvious application to piloting an aircraft through the three dimensions, but it is also relevant to navigating the course of a company. In both cases, the specific goal may be apparent, however, a sole focus on the objective can lead to "tunnel vision" and permit unforeseen hazards to emerge without having been previously considered.

Not every member of a crew may lose their situational awareness. It is important for all parties, regardless of standing, to shelve their ego and admit that a level of confusion is beginning to rise in their thought process. Similarly, the symptoms may be apparent to others. An extended period of silence in a dynamic situation, continually asking for instructions to be repeated and even a quizzical look on a face, can all be indicators to those around that situational awareness is being eroded.

Mentally stepping back to the "jumpseat" and pausing can offer breathing space and time in the surroundings. As a manager, it's essential that if this space is needed that one of your "co-pilots" is assigned the task of maintaining control of the flight path, or at sea-level, the day-to-day company operations. With mental capacity freed up by the delegation, the ability to look left and right above and behind, rather than straight ahead is enhanced.

Even with the best training, situational awareness can be lost. Overload, fatigue, unwanted distractions are just some of the hazards that can decrease our sense of orientation. If this happens, maintain control and, identify, verify and rectify. Once again, if this occurs, consider handing over to a co-pilot so that you can undertake a "lost procedure".

From the earliest cross-country training flights in a light aircraft, pilots are taught to prepare for the worst and as a fledgling aviator, getting lost is high on that list. As always, the priority is to keep flying the aircraft, as a loss of control makes being uncertain of one's position a moot point.

With the trajectory controlled and in a safe state, we need to look back to move forward. Where were we last assured of our position, what was the last positive landmark and time in the process that we can be assured of our position? What is the time now and where are we headed? This firstly may highlight how far from our planned track we have diverged.

Typically, when we navigate, we have a map – our plan – and anticipate the appearance of features presenting themselves in advance. We proceed step after step. When we are lost, we are no longer on our planned route, and we need to reverse the sequence or go "Big to Small", as aviators say.

Rather than waiting for a detail, like a railway line, on our map, we need to look for a sizeable landmark and then locate it on our map—something obvious and unmistakable, like a mountain, and then find it on the chart.

In a business sense, this may mean initially backtracking to the last meeting and retracing the steps since then, considering what time has elapsed. In going "Big to Small", the customer may need to be reidentified, and then their requirements considered. Moving smaller still, we may review their most recent correspondence, and then the point-of-contact, and so on until a full appreciation of the situation is regained. It is also worthwhile to remember that assistance may be available outside the cockpit. We learn to aviate, navigate and communicate in order of priority, so if doubt still exists, a pilot may seek help from air traffic control. A manager may need to seek assistance also.

In extreme situations, new pilots are trained that if they are hopelessly lost to conduct a precautionary landing at a suitable location before they run out of fuel or daylight. It is better to land the aircraft under control than be cornered into a situation when control is lost. History and accident investigations have shown that one of the main obstacles to making this difficult decision to land is not the pilot's ability, but their pride and ego.

Being aware of one's surroundings and being able to anticipate the challenges ahead are all aspects of being situationally aware. Those challenges may not always lie directly ahead, so the ability to step back and take in a broader perspective requires a conscious act that will become more natural with training and experience. Even then, situational awareness can be lost but it is not a time to panic - but to regroup. Identify the last known point and look for a conspicuous landmark. Working "Big to Small" from there will gradually restore orientation and allow the plan to again move forward in a controlled manner.

PEOPLE

Task Fixation, Saturation And Load Shedding

Having constructed a plan and even considered contingencies, a human trait that pilots can suffer from is being overly task-driven to an unhealthy level. It is essential that they have a task focus, but it cannot be all-consuming. In military circles, they speak of "target fixation" where the likes of a fighter pilot can become so fixated on the target that they risk colliding with the object rather than breaking off the attack on completion. In civilian circles, the term is task fixation, and it is not limited to aviation.

In a specific instance, the crew of Flight 401 in the section describing "The Danger of Distractions", became task fixated on the changing of a light bulb at the expense of monitoring the flight path and this led to the airliner crashing in the Florida Everglades. Similarly, in 1978, United Airlines Flight 173 was lost near Portland, Oregon, when an experienced crew failed to monitor their fuel status while they were addressing a perceived problem with the airliner's landing gear. All four engines of the Douglas DC-8 "flamed out" and, without power, the aircraft crashed short of the airport. Situations beyond the ordinary can teasingly elevate their true priority and draw our focus away from the primary task.

On a broader scale, a safe, on-time arrival at the destination is the standard goal for an airline pilot, but it too can become a fixation. A great deal of day-to-day satisfaction is derived from the efficient execution of a flight in the face of the numerous challenges and factors. Deep down, it is a source of professional pride. Unfortunately, that pride can distort judgement if it is allowed to gain too much influence.

If fixated, a delay may cause a rush in procedures before departure, threatening a crucial omission in a checklist. Airborne, despite the weather, task fixation may cause a pilot to attempt an approach to land when a diversion to another airport is the prudent, and even planned for, alternative.

The challenge of task fixation is the insidious nature of its onset. Fortunately, collaboratively working can provide a level of defence, although it is no guarantee as evidenced by the loss of Flight 401 in 1972. Fortunately, since then, in aviation circles at least, training and awareness of task fixation have vastly improved as have the means of communication allowing junior crew members to voice concern. Yet another benefit of open, two-way communication in the workplace.

Less subtle is the issue of "task saturation", and it is most definitely a threat to all undertakings, from piloting to parenting. It is the dreaded sense of being overwhelmed, with too much to do and insufficient time and resources to do it. Ever-increasing pressure that can manifest in frustration, hopelessness, forgetfulness, anger – a whole range of human emotions. In flight simulator sessions, pilots are often pushed towards the point of task saturation to observe their strategies when they begin to feel the onset of the symptoms as the world closes in.

The first step is recognition and, in the office or the flight deck, the input of others can assist with this. Unlike fixation, saturation is usually obvious to the individual – even if, at first, they try to deny it.

Next, it is vital to communicate that task saturation is taking hold to those that can assist. Again, ego and professional pride can delay such an admission, but as with most remedies, the earlier they are implemented, the quicker and more satisfactory the recovery will be.

With all parties aware of the situation, vigilance is increased once a problem has been identified. In airline operations, the priority is to ensure the safety of the aircraft while the issue is resolved. If coming into land, that may involve abandoning the approach and climbing to a safe altitude where a resolution can be achieved in the time that the remaining fuel permits. Subsequent relief can come from collaboration, or to use an aircraft systems term, "load shedding".

A saturated, overwhelmed pilot can assign tasks to the other to distribute the load more evenly. It may call for the other pilot to offer their assistance as the saturation may have reached a level to impede such a rational solution, or professional pride may again be influencing behaviour. Additionally, caution must be exercised not to overwhelm the party taking on the additional tasks. In some situations, the load may need to be shed over an even greater number of individuals.

Wanting to do well, take on more responsibility, take pride in one's work and achieve at a higher level are all admirable and positive qualities in the workplace. However, there remains the possibility of the silent creep of task fixation and the more obvious task saturation. Self-assessment or recognition by another is the first step towards returning to a state of balance. In a company with honest communication and a willingness to collaborate the burden of one can become the manageable task of the team.

PEOPLE

Roles, Responsibilities And Trust

A flight deck is a structured environment. From its ergonomic design, placing critical systems within both pilots reach and even designing switches to have certain tactile characteristics. The roles of the pilots are also well defined, down to the order of events and the language they use. And not least of which, their roles and responsibilities.

A role is a position assigned to an employee, such as a captain or co-pilot; their responsibilities are the specific tasks or duties that are involved. In airlines, the number of manuals describing how an operation, its aircraft and its people are required to function is numerous. Within them lies a section that details the specific responsibilities of each member of the crew, the chain of command and even which areas of the myriad flight deck controls are whose at any particular phase of flight. While the minute detail assigned to operating an aircraft may not be needed, all organisations and their people can benefit from clearly understanding their duties and where they fit into the greater entity.

Assigning roles within an organisational structure establishes the chain of command and the path of immediate accountability and reporting. Represented in an organisational diagram, it can also represent a potential career path to a junior rank and indicate possible resources to a manager. A co-pilot may aspire to be the captain in charge of training. In contrast, a captain can readily see that by passing a single instruction to the senior flight attendant in the cabin, a complex task involving several people can be put in place.

Defining responsibilities is important on several counts. Doing so reduces confusion through clarity it also avoids the inefficiency of overlapping and "doubling up" – which can further confuse. On occasions, domineering personalities can threaten to reverse the chain of command, or "cockpit gradient"; however, the definition of responsibilities provides a specific point of reference. Openly outlining responsibilities provides a level of accountability. It also guides those called to fill roles in another's absence or to plan a path of promotion or progression.

From a management perspective, responsibility has been conveyed as "Response – Ability". This describes that with responsibility comes the ability to choose how to respond. Particularly on the flight deck, there are procedures that a response must follow, but the choice of pace, timing and technique accompanies responsibility.

Defined roles and responsibilities will on occasions be varied, even in the most rigid organisational structure. There will also be times when roles can be exchanged. On the flight deck, pilots can alternate between which pilot is the actively "flying pilot" and the "support pilot". However, the ultimate responsibility for safe operation remains with the pilot-in-command. This is also the case when one party is training in a new role, and the trainer remains in the position of final authority. A situation that has led to confusion on some flight decks is when pilots of equal rank fill a range of roles. A training captain flying as a co-pilot, or a management pilot undertaking a check flight by a more junior captain are just a couple of examples.

Whenever a variation in roles and responsibilities exist, it must be documented, and the different roles understood. It is also valuable to reinforce the revised arrangement immediately before undertaking a task, ideally through a short briefing. If it is a temporary measure, then stating its duration and marking its termination will add to the clarity. Any new structure must be briefed with clarity and tact as varied roles will not always be popular but may be necessary for continuity and achievement of the task.

Underpinning all roles and responsibilities is the issue of trust. A successful, safe, and efficient flight deck and any organisation, requires trust to function. A captain needs to be able to trust that the engineer has been thorough when they have signed that an aircraft inspection is complete and that the load control office has loaded the aircraft correctly. Critically, the captain must trust that the co-pilot is fit to fly and competent. It is not possible to fill all roles or verify every detail, so in accepting overall responsibility, trust must be present. There are those captains and managers that will attempt to inject their influence into every aspect of the operation, and they are generally perceived as "micromanagers".

As a workplace, the flight deck has very clearly defined roles and responsibilities, and these serve as an aid to safety, efficiency, and communication. Each party understands their position intimately and possesses a clear picture of how that interacts with those around them. Even so, it has the flexibility to vary the roles and responsibilities but achieves this in an equally ordered and defined manner. Information is key to dispelling fear and confusion. The open communication of roles and responsibilities across an entire organisation removes ambiguity and replaces it with clarity. Trust is the other quality that allows a team to function smoothly and place the greater task as the priority.

PEOPLE

The Final Filter

"A superior pilot uses their superior judgment to avoid situations which require the use of their superior skill." A modern take on one of the great quotes of aviation, it is credited to test pilot and commander of Apollo 8, Colonel Frank Borman. And it is a philosophy that pilots strive for through a conservative outlook and an adherence to proven processes and techniques. Even so, aviation history books are filled with incidents when it still fell upon the pilot to be the final filter.

Well portrayed by James Reason's slices of Swiss Cheese are the holes through which hazards must slip to create a negative outcome. In this model, the airline crew is generally regarded as the final slice of cheese that can prevent an accident. It is a role that crews recognise they may be called upon to perform.

The readily quoted example is US Airways Flight 1549 when "Sully" performed the "Miracle on the Hudson", but there have been others. The uncontained engine failure of QANTAS QF32, a double-deck Airbus A380, saw the crew confronted by an unprecedented number of messages indicating systems failures and faults. Fifty tonnes over their maximum landing weight and with more than 400 lives on board, the crew safely nursed the crippled airliner to a safe landing. In both cases, they were events that could not be guarded against by operational procedures or rectified with a checklist. Beyond the scope of training, the crew had to deal with the situation that arose using their experience, skill and understanding at a level that exceeded any textbook.

QF32 and United 1549 were both fortunate to have highly experienced crews on board at the time of their events. Although beyond being merely fortunate, it can reflect the advantage of having highly competent people at the operational edge in any organisation. Such people can be recognised for a depth of knowledge beyond the bare minimum that may be required. A quality checking and training system caters for this in an airline and filters pilots from the day of potential recruitment to the day they retire. At regular intervals they are tested with scrutiny applied each time that a pilot upgrades to a higher rank or is trained on a different type of aircraft.

The benefits of such a system may not be immediately apparent and bear a high cost. However, it need only be called upon once in earnest to save an airline or company. For the individual at the coal face, it is a matter of personal pride and professionalism. It takes self-discipline to continue to train and prepare for the extraordinary event that may never eventuate. It takes equal measures of self-discipline to apply themselves to the process day after day with enthusiasm and thoroughness. Thus, avoiding the need to use their "superior skill".

Recognising that one is the final filter adds a perspective to decision making and when considering the "What ifs?" of a pre-mortem. Understanding that if it all goes wrong, the responsibility, and potentially the challenge to survive, will fall squarely upon the shoulders of the captain and the crew. And it may not even be a question of whether they are capable but whether the risk is worthwhile.

As a manager, or as a captain, there is the recognition that the final decision rests with them. It may not be life or death but that it has slipped through the preceding filters will generally suggest that the ramifications are significant. Here, the power of the pause and the actions of *identify, verify, and rectify* can provide a solid base from which to start.

Void of emotion, crews will make the assessment and plan to mitigate risk before such an event can ever take place, and this is a philosophy that can be adopted by any leader. Is there a strategy that can be employed to operate safely within the "edges of the envelope"? Even when this plan is available and adopted, there will be times when circumstances collide beyond the realm of probability, and that is when leaders of quality stand up to be counted.

Summary Of Techniques, Tactics And Strategy

DECISION MAKING.

G – Gather information from every available source.

R – Review the Information, discarding what is not relevant and prioritising what remains.

A – Analyse the information and mitigate against risk.

D – Decide and initiate a course of action.

E – Evaluate the course of action. Is it working? If not, action an alternate plan.

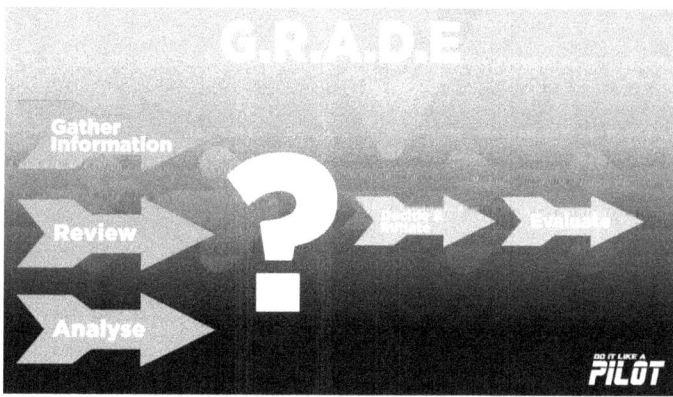

DEBRIEFING – FINDING THE GAPS.

G – Gather the information.
A – Assess the facts.
P – Perform a "Post-mortem"
S – Identify the shortfall between the outcome and the original goal.

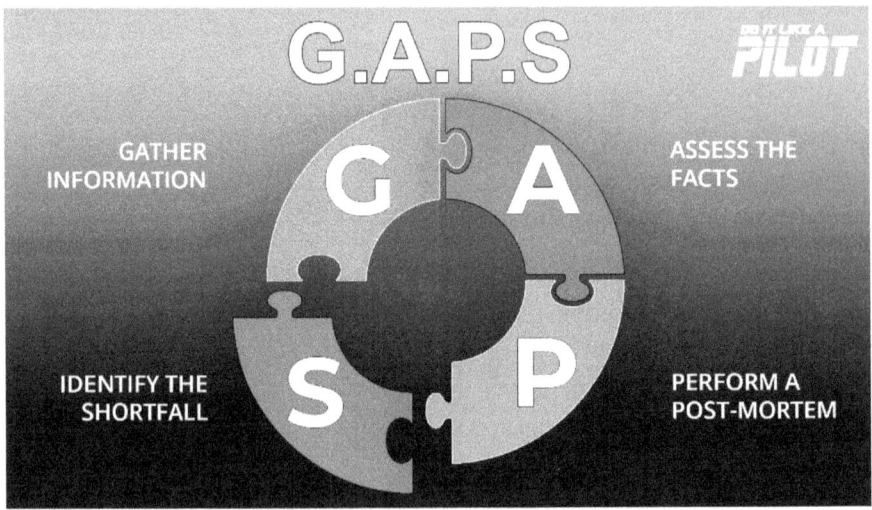

STOP – THE POWER OF THE PAUSE.

S – **S**top and Breathe.
T – **T**imeframe.
O – **O**ptions.
P – **Pl**an and Execute.

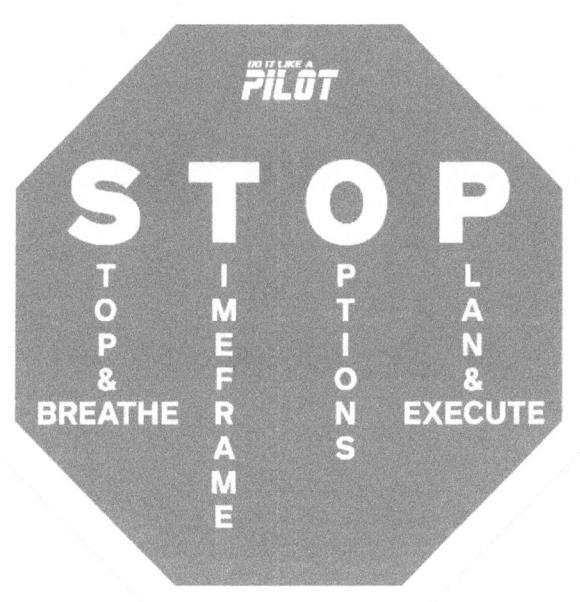

IDENTIFY – VERIFY – RECTIFY

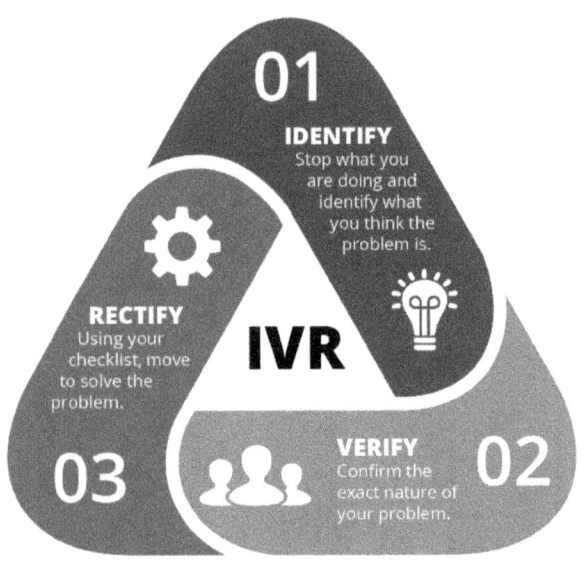

"MANAGING UPWARDS"

C – Convey Information.

A – Ask the question. "Do you know that we…?", "Are we going to…?"

I – "I" Statement. "I'm concerned …", "I'm not confident …", I'm not comfortable …"

R – Offer a Resolution. "Perhaps we could…", "Another option would be to…"

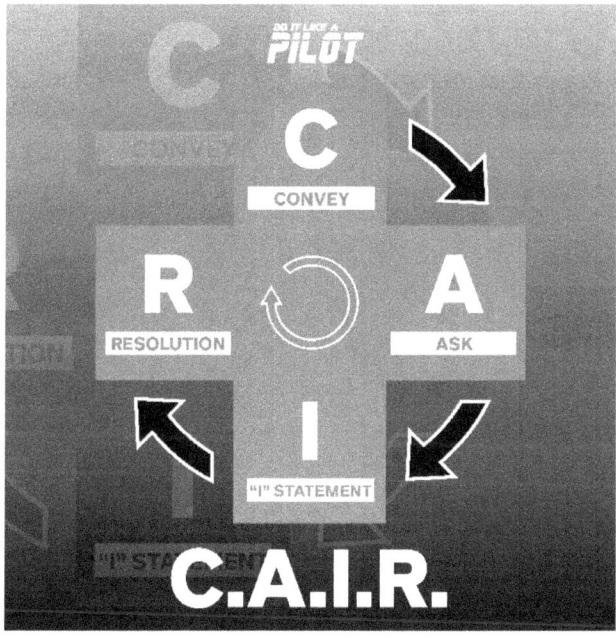

C.L.E.A.R

C – **Cadence**. Maintain an even, steady pace of speech.
L – **Language**. Use the correct **L**anguage.
E – **Efficient**. Be **E**fficient through minimum words and maximum listening.
A – **Audience**. Consider the **A**udience.
R – **Received**. Confirm the information has been **R**eceived.

WARNING SIGNS.

The NITS Brief.

N - **N**ature of the issue.
I - **I**ntentions.
T - **T**imeframe.
S - **S**pecial Instructions.

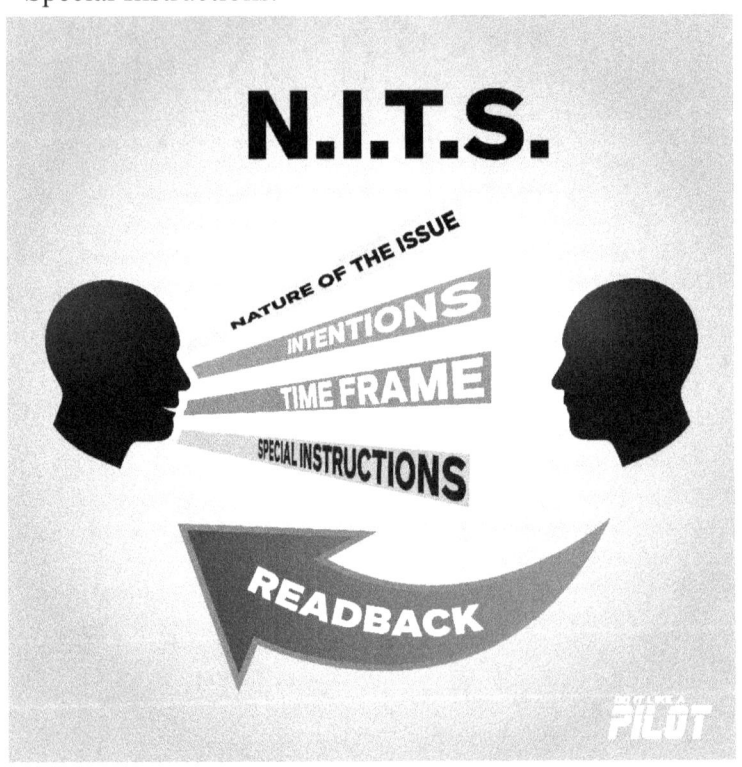

PART TWO

THE FRAMEWORK

INTRODUCTION

The "Do It Like A Pilot" Framework

The first part of this book unveiled a range of techniques, tactics and strategies that are routinely used by airlines and their pilots to safely and efficiently convey their passengers - systems that can also be applied to a range of non-aviation scenarios. In this second part, we shall outline a framework that can be overlaid upon an organisation or project to execute a plan. The framework offers a core structure, comprised of various stages and employing what we have read in part one regarding communications, processes and people.

The framework will be represented as a flight sequence, for the parallels that it draws to other organisations and undertakings. From the deeper planning and company culture well before the operation takes place to the need to review and report on completion. Underpinning the "flight" is the P.A.I.R. technique of *Planning – Advise – Initiate – Review and Report*.

Branching out from the standard framework will be the means to deal with issues when they arise. Whether a take-off or landing needs to be abandoned or coping with an unforecast issue through I.V.R, or the *"Identify – Verify – Rectify"* model.

The following words and diagrams can be referred to so that a seemingly complicated task can be broken down into stages and addressed. It is a proven methodology employed by air crews around the world every day to achieve sound results in what are complex machines operating in a dynamic natural and commercial environment.

FRAMEWORK

IDENTIFY VERIFY RECTIFY

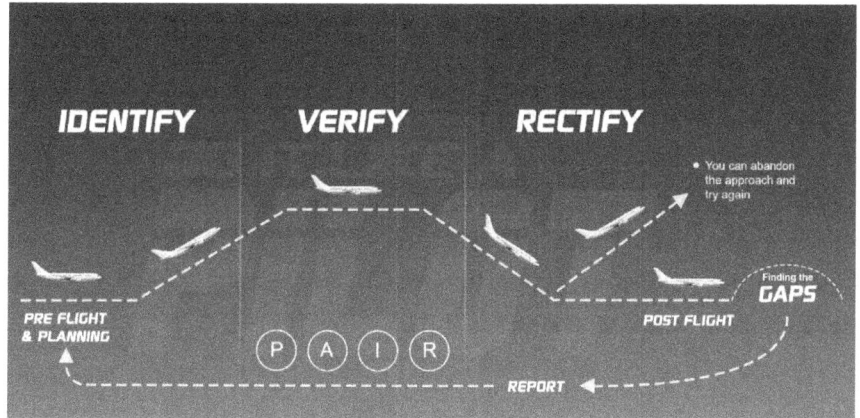

Identify. Verify. Rectify.

As discussed earlier, unless we take care in the wake of an incident, we may attend to the symptoms but overlook the real cause, allowing the same problem to resurface at a later date.

Recalling the "Swiss Cheese Model", Professor Reason drew a parallel to slices of Swiss Cheese, complete with holes, and each slice representing a point at which an action could have prevented the outcome. For an aircraft accident to occur, the holes in several slices of the cheese had to line up. The accident is prevented by a checklist catching an omission, or a standard procedure highlighting a digression. The pilots are effectively the final slices of cheese, the final filter.

Pilots use the term "non-normal", and as a term, it may seem clumsy, and it is. Logically, it means an occurrence that is out of the norm, which may, or may not, be life-threatening – yet.

And on occasions there may be multiple failures and warnings which require prioritisation. These complex events are impossible to mitigate against, so we need to adapt accordingly. In drastic situations such as QF32, there was a valid case in asking what do we have left? What do we have to work with? As opposed to the normal scenario of diagnosing the failure.

Utilising the *Identify – Verify – Rectify* process offers a "known" in a situation which may have its challenges among flashing warnings and ringing bells. Training kicks in, pilots stop, take a breath and allow logic to override emotion. They ensure the aircraft is in a safe state, they communicate the issue with the other pilot and confirm their understanding. They can then, together, commence at a common point that they both know and understand.

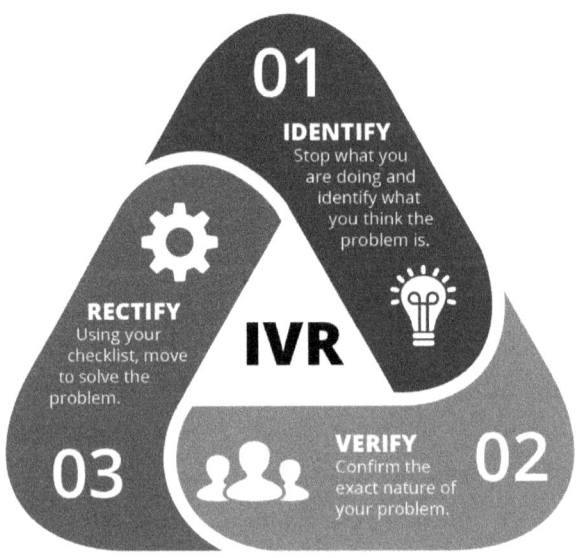

Identify – Verify – Rectify.

After ensuring that the aircraft, organisation, or personnel are in a safe situation, our first action in addressing an issue, be it an anomaly or an emergency, is to *identify*. A variety of means can achieve identification before the problem arises, should we have strategies in place. Addressing issues before they manifest as something more threatening is the ideal situation in an organisation and in flight. Company procedures, reporting channels, training and checklists are some of the preventative measures that can be in place. Even so, there will be occasions when undesired events can still occur, and a more immediate response is called for.

The triggers for identifying a problem can be subtle, or obvious, just as an aircraft can have advisory, cautionary and warning systems. In an organisation, the first sign may be a missed deadline, a customer complaint, absenteeism, or divergence from company procedures or culture. It may be the breakdown of equipment on the factory floor.

Recognising that a problem exists and then effectively communicating the issue sets the IVR process in motion. The emphasis on effectively communicating means that the correct people are made aware and immediate feedback is received to confirm that they understand the problem.

The second part of the framework is to *verify*. There are several management models in existence that portray an apparent path as a triangle, or a pyramid, ascending to an apex. They move from identifying a problem straight to trying to fix the problem. In the methodology of "*Identify – Verify – Rectify*", it calls for a verification stage, represented as a plateau, rather than a peak. Why? A plateau is a pause to verify that the issue has been correctly identified *before* pursuing a course of action.

To immediately initiate a plan without a chance to think it through is fraught with danger. There are very few instances that call for an immediate response, and yet the ramifications of an incorrect plan can prove fatal.

Even in the critical scenario where an airliner's engine fails or catches fire just as it lifts off from the runway, there is a pause before the plan is enacted. Firstly, the aircraft has to be kept flying safely and under control, even if it only just climbing into the sky. Only then do the pilots positively identify which engine has failed and set about shutting it down. Thus, preventing it from creating further damage or hampering the aircraft's ability to climb. In contrast, let's consider a hasty reaction. In the first instance, the crew become all-consumed by the warning lights and bells and disregard the primary task of continuing to fly the aircraft. The aircraft impacts the ground. Alternatively, even if they continue to fly the aircraft safely but rush into shutting down the failed engine without carefully confirming which engine is the culprit. They now effectively have two "failed" engines, and again, the aircraft impacts the ground.

We have examined the benefits of "pausing" and "verifying" earlier in this book, and that is why the IVR model more closely resembles a flat-topped mesa than a pyramid. In verifying, we pause to verify that we are looking at the correct issue and confirm this with an independent party, be that a team member, another manager, or in some cases an external consultant. The timeframe for rectification can then be discussed – is it a critical failing needing immediate attention, or minor fault that can be addressed over a longer-term? All the while, we are avoiding "task fixation" and cross-checking that the rest of our organisation is still "flying" in a safe environment.

The third component, when we have positively identified and verified the problem, is to *"rectify"*. So often we want to leap into fixing a problem, it's human nature. However, as we've seen in "Identify" and "Verify", haste can lead to undesired outcomes in both the short and longer terms. Furthermore, taking the time to verify the problem, the subsequent plan to fix it can be commenced with confidence. Duties can be assigned, with the first being who is to keep flying the aircraft. A positive hand-over and take-over of responsibilities may need to occur before proceeding.

Rectification can also be approached in a clear and structured manner in the form of the next topic - **P.A.I.R.** - **P**lan. **A**dvise. **I**nitiate. **R**eview and **R**eport. (PAIR is the focus of the next topic.)

Keeping to the theme of this book by keeping it simple, when presented with a problem, *Identify – Verify – Rectify*. A three-part framework that provides a means by which we can implement the effective strategies used by flight crews to address issues when they arise - on the ground and in the air.

FRAMEWORK

P.A.I.R.
Plan — Advise — Initiate — Review & Report

Whether overseeing an entire project, or addressing a specific problem, recalling the P.A.I.R framework will offer a solid foundation from which to build. Concise in its form, it can be expanded as needed to cover a range of situations. Importantly, embedded in aviation but often overlooked elsewhere, the ongoing process of "review and report" is vital.

Planning is achieved within the cultural and procedural construct of the organisation. Under this umbrella a goal is agreed upon. In the short term, it may be resolving an isolated problem, or in the long term, introducing new equipment. Either way, the plan begins with a goal.

It is important to address any threats or additional considerations from the outset as, given time, they may escalate in scale or arise when we are less equipped to deal with them. The "pre-mortem" and its style of open discussion and "What Ifs?" allows adverse scenarios to be considered from the unconventional perspective of pessimism. Once identified, the threats can be verified and assessed for their probability and consequence, that is to say, their level of risk. From this point a mitigating strategy can be advised.

Having considered the initial negative eventualities, a suitable strategy can be devised - this is the core of the plan. However, the pre-mortem may have identified ongoing risks to the project, so contingencies may need to be put in place – alternate plans that can be executed, possibly with minimal notice. At this stage, responsibilities are assigned and the limiting parameters of the project need to be considered - the "Go. No-Go." point for commencement and any critical limits during the execution. The base plan has now been formulated.

Advise. Armed with a considered plan, the next stage is to communicate that plan to all of the stakeholders, both within and beyond the organisation. From management level to the most junior rank at the operational level, the plan needs to be conveyed and, most importantly, understood. Equally critical is that the communication is two-way with a means of receiving feedback as there may be previously unforeseen issues raised by other stakeholders that lie outside the original planning process.

Initiate. With the plan finalised and roles clearly defined it is time to initiate and execute the plan. From the outset, it is imperative to compare progress against the plan. This will advise the team if it is approaching any of the project's limits, calling into play either a modification, a contingency plan, or in the worst case, an abandonment before the stakes become too high. If needed the model of "*Identify - Verify - Rectify*" can be actioned to address any issues and in turn, P.A.I.R can form part of that rectification process, albeit more likely on a smaller, more timely, scale.

Review and Report. This final step in P.A.I.R. is vital and can flourish in a mature organisation with a "just" culture and a sound reporting system. Any flight or project should exist under a constant state of review and report. The review process identifies trends and these trends may need to be modified with action, particularly if they are approaching pre-defined limits.

On completion of a project, great or small, an organisation should review the outcome and compare it to the original goal from the planning phase. Negative and positive variations should be reported to highlight shortcomings and reinforce successes. Armed with this information, it can be reported to affect change for the future. Through this honest, open communication and at times, self-criticism, organisations stand to make substantial positive progress. The G.A.P.S technique is well suited to identifying any differences, or "gaps".

Completion of a project is not a time to rest on laurels, it is a time to review and report while the details are still readily at hand. Successful organisations share a culture that encourages honest feedback from all ranks without fear of retribution. Review and report is a critical step towards improvement.

P.A.I.R is another tool in the leader's toolbox that if trained within an organisation can form a style of "Standard Operating Procedure". All members of the team expect that after the plan is devised, stakeholders will be advised. If this doesn't occur, an expectation hasn't been met and a possible hazard has slipped through a hole in the Swiss

Cheese model. Similarly, at the conclusion, the team will expect that a debriefing and a review of the project will take place and that elements, good and bad, will be reported.

As part of the greater framework, P.A.I.R is invaluable. Simple to recall and logical to follow.

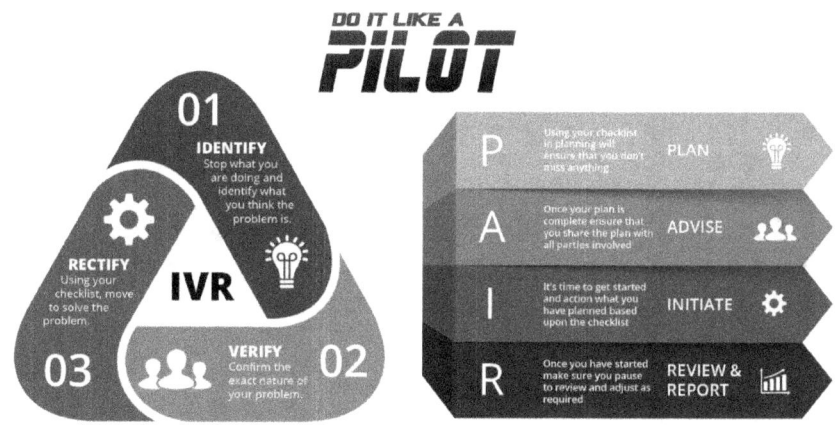

FRAMEWORK

The "Do It Like A Pilot" Framework

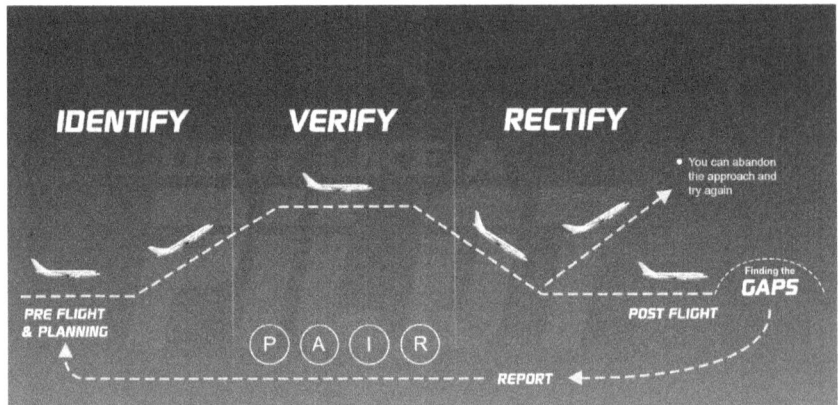

Drawing together all the techniques, tactics and strategies examined so far and overlaying the Identify - Verify - Rectify and P.A.I.R. models we can arrive at our overall, "Do it Like a Pilot", or DILAP, framework. Explained in terms of a flight, this summary draws parallels to any organisation and can be implemented. And it begins well before any project ever takes flight.

The tone for any organisation is set at the upper level of management. It is here that the "Mission Statements" are written, the vision is conjured, and the example is set. This is where "culture" is born.

An organisation's culture must encompass every stakeholder, from the boardroom to the basement. At all levels, the customs, behaviours and outlook must be understood and exercised. Authenticity in the pursuit of a healthy culture is vital, while insincerity can lead to a culture becoming toxic. Within the most respected airlines, the commitment to safety and professionalism is not merely an internal company concept, it is on show and even used in marketing.

Two aspects of their culture that set noted airlines apart are possessing a "just culture" and promoting a culture of reporting without recrimination. In a just culture, where genuine errors are not punished but actively addressed and learned from, a reporting system can thrive. Events once swept under the carpet and left to manifest, are captured, and examined. Trends are monitored and training initiated, and procedures amended as needed. In a superior organisation, the culture has matured so that stakeholders will self-report their errors. Similarly, feedback is encouraged from all levels of the organisation.

At the same senior level of management where culture is initiated, long term plans and goals for the organisation are drawn up. Just as airline crew will "pre-mortem" possible unfavourable outcomes, there is benefit in any management taking a pessimistic perspective and asking, "What if?" in advance. By doing so, their outlook can be more balanced, and strategies can be put in place to counter any potential threats. In the worst case, the pre-mortem may uncover an aspect of the plan that makes it unviable. This is far better than once the plan has been initiated. It is best to know if the destination airport is closed before the wheels ever leave the ground!

With culture, planning, and a reporting system in place, the day of departure looms. Whether a major project or a small interim program, a briefing is best undertaken. Timely, relevant and targeted, the briefing will outline the plan, threats and considerations and any contingency planning that is in place. Any non-negotiable "Go. No-Go" points will be agreed upon, and if it becomes apparent that the project is approaching that point, it should be reinforced that "whoever sees it – calls it." Finally, roles and responsibilities will be re-confirmed and as with all forms of communication, the "feedback loop" is open for any member of the team to raise an issue. The project is now cleared for take-off.

It's dusk as the brakes are released, and the aircraft accelerates rapidly towards flight. The sensation is exciting, but regardless, the crew must remain focused and monitor their "V1" – their decision speed. With the wings now generating lift the airliner lofts off and into the sky. The passengers and airline depend upon the professional execution of the task by the crew. A project taking flight is a relief after long and intensive planning, but the task now requires equal commitment now it is airborne.

The departure and climb are a busy time for the crew. The aircraft has to be reconfigured from a machine seeking to get airborne to becoming a vehicle with a very specific task and all manner of possible variables ahead. Well clear of the ground and headed in the right direction, the captain will review the departure in an open forum with the crew. As a manager, humility is exercised, offering up any personal oversights during the recent departure before inviting further insights, criticisms or positive input from the crew. Any noteworthy points are considered for their impact on the continued operation and recorded for submission into the reporting system. The crew has already completed a cycle of P.A.I.R. They have planned, advised, initiated and reviewed.

Flying straight and level in the cruise is routinely the most straightforward segment of the flight. After the effort of launching a project, a team must continually monitor its progress, not allowing the relative calm to allow complacency to creep on. The progress is tracked and compared to the original plan – has more fuel been used than planned? On schedule, or behind? In a quiet moment, the discussion may turn to a hypothetical "What if?" They may gather the latest information relating to their alternate destination – just in case. In addition to revalidating the earlier contingency planning, considering a problematic scenario keeps the team in a prepared mental state.

Flying along one of the highways in the sky, known as an airway, Air Traffic Control comes on the radio, offering a straight-line route that will "cut the corner" and shave off miles, to be flown, fuel to be used and with minutes to be saved – it's a kind offer. The crew acknowledges the offer and then – pauses. They consider the savings but notice the red "blip" on the screen of their weather radar as it sweeps the horizon. The route is shorter but by diverging from the original plan will put the aircraft on course to fly into the thunderstorms that are flashing outside. They all agree and politely decline the offer. Sometimes a straight line is not the best option, and frequently such decisions are required by teams operating under a "decentralised command".

More time passes, and the destination grows closer – on plan and on time. All is right with the world. Until an amber message illuminates – there is a problem and regardless of rank, whoever sees it calls it. One of the pilots immediately announces their control of the aircraft and verifies that it is in a safe state. A little startled – there is time for a pause – and a deep breath. The pilots start a clock to keep an appreciation of time—another breath. The mind is now clear.

Identify – Verify – Rectify.

The problem is *identified* by one pilot and confirmed by the other. It is an air conditioning issue, not major, but with the potential to escalate. It is not a contingency that was planned for or expected. The aircraft still has altitude, adequate fuel, and time. It is safe. The problem is *verified,* and the appropriate checklist is completed. The aircraft is unaffected although it now has a reduced air conditioning capability.

The situation can now be *rectified,* and a decision made by Gathering all available information from all available sources. The captain hands over control to the co-pilot and calls the Cabin Manager to enquire if any smoke or smell is coming through the air conditioning system – there is not. Next, the latest weather and information for the available airports, including the planned destination, is accessed. All airports are available and fine. They contact maintenance support and flight operations via satellite link. They have no further information to provide but inform the captain that the engineers at the destination will be advised.

The captain comes back to the crew to "G.R.A.D.E" the situation, but first, the co-pilot offers a mini-brief to update the captain's situational awareness of the aircraft's status. Distractions, even those in the best interest of the operation, can erode the team's S.A. With everyone "in the loop" the G.R.A.D.E begins.

The gathered information is shared and reviewed. Nothing is preventing the original plan from going ahead. Although a pre-mortem is conducted to analyse the situation. Should another air-conditioning fault occur, the aircraft may lose cabin pressurisation and have to descend. Burning more fuel flying at that lower level, they would not make the destination.

In the immediate sense, nothing needs to be rectified further, but risk must still be mitigated against and contingencies catered for. A decision must be made.

To do so, the crew consider P.A.I.R with the available information. They plan to continue to the destination, although they have closer alternate airports available should the other air conditioning system fail. They advise the Cabin Manager of the situation and ask for the cabin crew to be briefed and report anything unusual regarding the air conditioning system in the cabin. This is a NITS briefing. Flight operations are also advised of the plan by satellite link.

The plan is initiated, with the flight continuing as planned but with data relating to the other airports at the ready. The decision is reviewed and the crew review, in advance, the checklists and procedures to descend and divert if needed. The G.R.A.D.E process is completed with a final evaluation of the decision and continued monitoring of progress versus plan.

The remainder of the flight is without event. Another briefing is conducted in a concise and timely manner prior to arriving at the destination. Threats and considerations and the parameters of a "stable approach" are discussed. Considered are the actions in a "go-around", and the amount of fuel onboard, in terms of time and options. Feedback and questions are invited, but none are forthcoming.

The arrival is flown, and the original goal of a safe and efficient flight has been achieved, despite potential problems arising enroute. They were identified, verified and rectified utilising the G.R.A.D.E. model for decision-making, P.A.I.R for initiating and reviewing a plan and N.I.T.S for advising the crew.

With the passengers disembarked, the crew will gather to assess the flight using the G.A.P.S technique. They will discuss and analyse any positive and negative aspects that need reporting or reinforcement. Again, the captain will lead with humility, offering any improvements that could be made on a personal level. The review will be summarised, and any necessary reporting will be completed. This report will generate a response from the organisation and potentially prompt change. Not every tactic and strategy will be employed on every flight. However, some, such as G.A.P.S. will always occur, allowing the reporting process to lead to future improvement.

By observing the diagram that accompanies this section, the progress of a flight, or a project, can be seen through the "Do it Like a Pilot" framework. It can then be translated and overlaid onto any organisation, with its various techniques, tactics and strategies to circumvent and address issues as they arise.

Employing the strategies used by respected airlines, an organisation will gain a sound, authentic culture whose regular processes create an expectation, or Standard Operating Procedures, that highlight any divergence. And when obstacles inevitably appear in their path, the organisation can adapt and in a measured fashion and consider alternate plans in a timely fashion.

There is no need for panic. There is only a pause. Check the ego. Check the emotions.

Appreciate the situation and don't become distracted.

Take command and lead with humility.

Identify - Verify - Rectify.

Do it like a pilot.

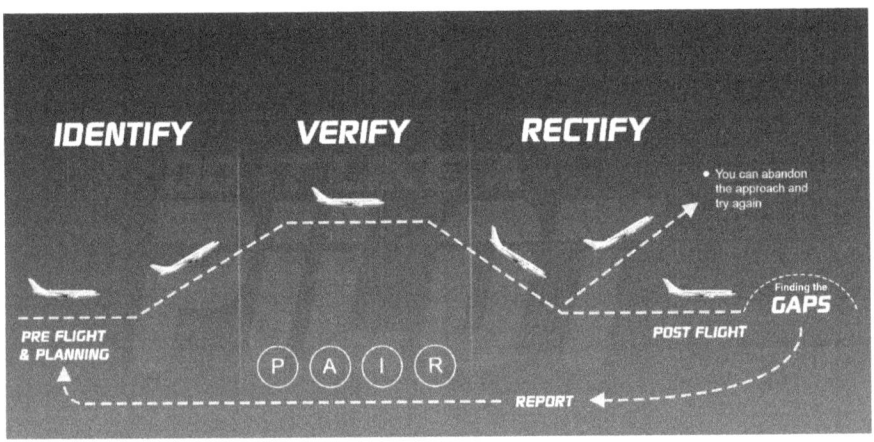

One Last Word

Thank you for reading, "Do it Like a Pilot".
You can find more resources, bringing flight deck skills to life and business at the website - Do it Like a Pilot.
And my other books...
The Practical Pilot. (Paperback and eBook)
Boeing 747. Queen of the Skies. Reflections from the Flight Deck. (Paperback and eBook)
'Without Precedent' Fighter Pilot, Commando. (Hardcover, Paperback and eBook)
'50 Tales of Flight' (Paperback and eBook)
'50 More Tales of Flight' (Paperback and eBook)
'Solo Flight' One Pilot's Aviation Adventure around Australia (Paperback and eBook)
'Down to Earth' A Fighter Pilot's Experiences of surviving Dunkirk, the Battle of Britain, Dieppe and D-Day. (Grub Street Publishing. 2007)

Aviation is an ongoing process of accumulating experience and knowledge that never ends.
Thanks again and safe flying.
Owen

***

ABOUT THE AUTHOR

A former paramedic, Owen Zupp is an award-winning writer, published author and commercial pilot with more than 20,000 hours of flight time. In addition to his Masters Degree of Aviation Management, Owen has flown all manner of machines, from antique biplanes to Boeings and Airbuses and shared the journey with readers around the world in his books and a variety of publications.

The son of a decorated fighter pilot, Owen was born into aviation. His flying career has taken him from outback Australia to the rugged mountain ranges of New Guinea, the idyllic islands of Micronesia and across the oceans of the world. He has served as a Chief Flying Instructor, Chief Pilot and an Approved Test Officer, holding the authority to issue and renew pilot licences and ratings.

Whether witnessing rocket launches from 40,000 feet or circumnavigating a continent for charity in a tiny two-seat training aircraft, Owen has cherished every minute aloft. Flight is not merely his profession, it is his passion, and through "Do it Like a Pilot" he is sharing those skills with a wider audience than ever before.

Acknowledgements

My heartfelt thanks to every pilot, flight instructor, mentor, check and training captain that I have encountered and every fellow enthusiast that I have chatted with over a coffee – thank you. As a pilot I am the by-product of all of your lessons and input.

To my wife, Kirrily, and our children, thank you for your enthusiasm and patience in equal measures. And as an airline pilot, Kirrily also deserves credit for casting a critical eye over the manuscript.

To my mother and father, thank you for every ounce of advice that you gave me year in, year out. As a son, brother, father and friend I am the by-product of all of your lessons and input.

To Rob Brus, for motivating me to finally write this book and his support through the process.

And without you, the readers, this book would be merely a voice in the wilderness. Your emails, reviews and kind words continue to inspire me to write. You can never underestimate the impact that your support has made to my journey as a writer. Thank you.

Cheers
Owen

www.ingramcontent.com/pod-product-compliance
Lightning Source LLC
Chambersburg PA
CBHW070559010526
44118CB00012B/1386